BUY THE DAMN COFFEE

Buy the Damn Coffee
How Women of Faith Ditch Guilt and Shame Around Money

Janine Mix

©2024 All Rights Reserved. No portion of this book may be reproduced, stored in a retrieval system, or transmitted in any form or by any means- electronic, mechanical, photocopy, recording, scanning, or other-except for brief quotations in critical reviews or articles without the prior permission of the author.

Published by Game Changer Publishing

Paperback ISBN: 978-1-964811-89-5
Hardcover ISBN: 978-1-964811-06-2
Digital ISBN: 978-1-965653-41-8

www.GameChangerPublishing.com

DEDICATION

To the woman who wants to make more income and impact.
Financial freedom starts with you, one trailblazer at a time.

A GIFT FOR YOU

Just to say thank you for buying and reading my book, I would like to give you a few free bonus gifts and resources! You can download these gifts by scanning the QR code below.

For Free Gifts, Scan the QR Code:

Buy the Damn Coffee

*How Women of Faith Ditch Guilt
and Shame Around Money*

Janine Mix

GC GAME CHANGER PUBLISHING

www.GameChangerPublishing.com

Table of Contents

Introduction 1

Chapter 1 – "Poverty Mind" versus "Prosperity Mind" 11

Chapter 2 – Common Money Myths 27

Chapter 3 – 3 Money Influencers 51

Chapter 4 – Not Your Fault 69

Chapter 5 – No One Will Save You 79

Chapter 6 – Every Mission Requires Money 97

Chapter 7 – Men, Marriage, and Money 111

Chapter 8 – Your Kingdom Assignment 137

Chapter 9 – Becoming a Trailblazer 151

Conclusion – This is Your Story 177

References 189

Introduction

I can remember the exact moment I knew something in my life had to change drastically.

Sitting in my closet in my studio apartment, I was on the phone with my sister. She was walking me through my weekly budget. I was crying, explaining how it was impossible for me to pay my bills, especially after the $80 parking ticket I had just gotten. My alarm didn't go off before 7 a.m., and that's when all the cars needed to be moved off the street so the street sweep could come by. I was living in Los Angeles, trying to "make it" as an actress. For most of us out there, that means we have a full-time waitressing job, a few side hustles, and are broke as a joke while still barely able to make an audition.

Let me not skim past why I was sitting in my closet. You see, our building had its very own creepy stalker, and he lived right next to me. He would torment a few of us girls in the building. He'd leave strange things on our doorstep, watch us through his cracked door when we got home, and harass us by covering our peephole on the door, yelling, slipping notes through our door, and knocking at all hours of the night. Our landlord didn't have enough substantial "proof" to do anything about it. So when he wasn't home, I would sneak to my apartment, turn off all the lights, and hide in my closet so he couldn't hear me. Sad, I know, but this was my reality.

Once a week, my sister would talk me through all my "envelopes" and categories for the month, which always reminded me how broke I was, how bad I was with money, and how—no matter how hard I worked—I would never have enough. I was the only one I knew who paid their own way through college at a private university, the only one working two to three jobs while going to college, and the only one of my peers who was paying $1,200 a month in student loans right out of college. If you knew me in my early days of living in Los Angeles, all I ever did was work. Having two to three jobs was normal for me, but no matter how hard I worked, I just couldn't get ahead.

No joke, I would sleep in my car because there wasn't any parking when I got off work at 2 a.m., and I couldn't afford another ticket. In L.A., the fines doubled for multiple offenses.

No matter how hard I tried, I knew I was going to hear my sister say, "You don't have enough money," no matter how many times I told my friends I couldn't go to the movies with them, no matter how many times I had to pass on dinner nights, no matter how many endless times I would be in the line at Starbucks with knots in my stomach, thinking about all the empty "envelopes" at home, the reality was I was still broke.

How do people get ahead? I had no idea. Was this it for me? Was I going to suffer for the next 30 years, paying off $120,000 in student loan debt and living in an apartment I was afraid to even go home to?

I was confused. I did everything "they" told me to. I got good grades, went to a good college, graduated, and got a job—all of this just to live miserably. All the fun in my life was removed just so I could roll over an extra $100 to pay off my debt. *Only after I have struggled like this for 30 years will I finally be debt-free?* I thought. *Then, can I start enjoying life?*

One thing you should know about me is I've always gone against the grain. When they zig, I zag. I love pushing the status quo. I just didn't realize that I was also a people pleaser. My whole life, I have been trying to earn the love of others through my achievements. So, what my parents, family, and friends saw as the best path for me, I did. But sitting on the floor in the closet of my tiny studio apartment at that moment, I knew that if I was going to live a full life, travel the world, and pursue my dreams, it wasn't going to happen like this. I knew there had to be a better way.

Like most overnight success stories, it would be another three years of struggling, losing my job, being on unemployment, deferring my loans (*not recommended*), and moving into a brand-new apartment infested with cockroaches, that I would finally take the biggest leap of faith yet.

I hit the reset button on my life. I moved out of a state I lived in for 23 years to a place I had never been, with a guy I had only just started dating, without a job, and no ties or connections whatsoever.

But this isn't a Cinderella story where the prince sweeps her off her feet and saves her from her evil debt sister (see what I did there?). This is a story of two people who were tired. Tired of being in hours of traffic, tired of being broke, with a deep sense that God had something better planned for us. We knew it wasn't in Los Angeles. We knew there had to be a better way that didn't include cutting up credit cards, broken budgets, and waiting until retirement to start living. Leaving California allowed us to keep our heads above water so we could start plotting a life together on our terms.

The Leap of Faith

Now here I was, moving to a state I had never been to, with no job, no place to live, not knowing a single person, $120,000 in debt, and less than $2,000 in my bank account after I had sold everything I owned in L.A. to move—for a boy.

What was I thinking?!

I'll tell you what I was thinking. I was 24. I was making good money working in retail but still had nothing to show for it. I had nothing to lose and everything to lose at the same time. But I knew one thing: there was just no way I was going to be able to pay off $120,000 of debt by cutting out lattes, rolling over a few hundred dollars of extra money I just didn't have, continuing to work two jobs and a side hustle for the next 30 years, and only then be able to retire, start living my life and travel the world.

Luckily, Ryan and I had the same idea. We knew there had to be a better way.

Our daily motto was, *"Life doesn't have to suck while we work towards our financial goals."*

It wasn't long until we both agreed that real estate would change our lives the fastest. But how was I going to get into more debt when I already bore the weight of so much? Oh, and what about the fact that we had no money? And Ryan's credit was shot. And we had no contacts or role models or any idea what we were doing. It was a terrible time to start investing in real estate, but we went for it. Then Ryan got fired. We were both broke and now he was unemployed. We buckled down even harder. We had a few months until his unemployment ran out, and I had a decent job to tide us over. This was it. This was the moment we could stop being victims of our lives, take a leap of faith, and go *all in!*

Did our families think we were crazy?

Yes!

Did I sign a mortgage with someone I wasn't married to yet?

Yes!

Did we borrow money from a credit card to rehab the project?

Yes!

Did we lose sleep most nights, hoping we hadn't made a mistake?

Yes!

I won't get into all the details of our first deal. But I will say with that first property, I was able to pay off $80,000 of my student loan debt in a few short years instead of 30. Taking that leap of faith at one of the lowest points in our lives was one of the best things we have ever done.

The real shift for us wasn't cutting up our credit cards or cutting out coffee. The secret was to stop focusing on what we didn't have and instead focus on money coming in and learning how to multiply that money.

We started to use debt and credit cards as leverage to purchase more real estate—because, remember, we had no money. During this time, we also started to get really good with credit card hacking for free travel. It was one of our goals not to wait until retirement to travel, and we made a promise to each other to go on one big trip every year. The only way to do that when we didn't have substantial cash flow coming in was to get really smart with maximizing the spending we were already doing in our personal lives and business. We learned how to trade points for travel without paying a penny of interest. We haven't paid for international flights in almost a decade because we learned to use credit cards to our advantage.

Some people might say, "You're stupid for using credit cards!" or "If you have ever been or currently are in debt with credit cards, you should just cut them up and never use them again!"

But that's like saying someone who is a bad driver should just never drive again. It's not realistic to expect someone to sell their car, never drive again, and only take other forms of transportation for the rest of their lives. A more realistic solution is to become a better driver by learning the rules of the road, practicing different skills like parallel parking, and learning more about the features of your vehicle so you can become more experienced with it.

Now, *could* we have cut out coffee, saved up some money, and just put our own cash into real estate? Sure. But we had no money, and going about it that way would have taken a lot longer to get where we wanted to go.

If you were to cut out coffee every day for the rest of your life and invest the $5 into modest stocks, the experts say you would have a million dollars in your portfolio by the time you are 65. Which sounds great, but:

- I am a better human being with coffee—you with me?
- $1 million at 65 isn't enough money to retire, given inflation and the costs of senior care.
- There is no guarantee that you'll even live to 65, which means your *entire* coffee-less life would have been for nothing.

And FYI, if we are strictly talking about investing, $1 million in 20 to 30 years isn't a very good return on investment.

So we *could* scrimp every penny, never go on dates, stay at our jobs, never start businesses until we have the cash, or invest in real estate only when we've saved enough for a down payment—and if there is money when we get to an older age, finally get to travel the world and enjoy the fruits of our labor.

This was just not the life we desired to live. For us, we knew we weren't promised tomorrow. We wanted to travel while we were young, able-bodied, and could experience crazy adventures without limiting our view to the window of a tour bus. We wanted to have enough money to retire before we got to 40, and we certainly didn't want to work for anyone else, which left collecting social security or relying on a company 401(k)–a weak and entirely risky retirement plan for us.

We considered the risks of both sides, and we took a leap we have never regretted since.

My point in sharing this is that there are other ways to use money, and certain kinds of debt *can* help get you the results you are looking for faster. Do you need to know how to manage money? Of course! Do you need to have a grip on your spending so you don't spiral down a very expensive debt hole by buying stupid things you can't afford? Duh.

Do you need to be willing to take some calculated risks? Absolutely! For us, the risks of counting on a job and our employer to provide for us for the next 30 years were greater than starting something of our own. Ryan had just been fired from his job unexpectedly, and the company I had been employed at for seven years closed its doors a few years after I left. There are no guarantees, and relying on our jobs gave us a false sense of security.

It dawned on me that financial freedom is different for everyone. Who decided that being debt-free is synonymous with being financially free? Who says you need to have [X] amount of dollars in your bank account to say you are financially free? That amount is different for everyone. For others, the idea of financial freedom is simply having a good-paying job and benefits. Some people never want to owe any money to anyone, and that's their freedom. Some people want to be able to buy a private jet. Some want to be their own boss and clock in on their own time. You see, everyone's version of financial freedom is different, and it can only be defined by you. The true challenge is actually defining it.

Most people haven't even thought about what they would do when they reach financial freedom, have you? Have you thought about what your average day would look like without having to worry about where the next payday is coming from? If money was no object, where would you be living? What does your dream house look like? Do you want to travel more? Where would you go? What activities would you do? Can you see your kids laughing and enjoying themselves as they make sandcastles on the beach of some Caribbean island? For some of you reading this, just by reflecting on a few of these questions, you have allowed your mind to cast a vision for what a life beyond bills would be like... maybe for the first time. If you don't take the time to actually cast a clear vision of your goals, dreams, and God's purpose for your life, how will you ever know when you have arrived?

Most people say they want to be financially free but haven't dreamed past paying off their credit cards. Most people say when they make more they want to give back, but they don't have a specific amount, organization, or cause in mind that will help motivate them. Most people want to pay off their house or buy their dream home, but they don't even think about how many rooms it has or the style of home, nor do they have any idea of what the cost of the house or mortgage would be. If you don't know what you want, I can promise you that you won't be motivated enough to go after it. Benjamin Franklin says, "If you fail to plan, you are planning to fail."

If you don't have a plan or vision, you'll adopt someone else's. I believe there are people preaching a version of financial freedom that is actually scaring us into more poverty. These are the people who tell you to shop at thrift stores, cut coupons, skip your lattes, drive cheap cars for the next 20 years, and eat a cheap diet of rice and beans. While these *might* be strategies for the short term, by continuously focusing on these strategies, you are shutting off your mind's ability to see another path and often building habits of scarcity that become your identity.

I've seen so many cases where someone has worked tirelessly to get out of their tough financial circumstance at all costs, only to be met with more fear of spending or enjoying money than when they started. They've adopted the idea that financial freedom requires massive sacrifices, some of which could be at the expense of their mental and physical well-being. They believe they should never buy a new car or it would be financially irresponsible even if their income could afford it. There's a crippling fear that they might go backward to the place of financial hardship, which often overshadows the realization of their new and improved circumstances. This is what I mean by being scared into scarcity and the poverty mindset. Our money identity has more of an impact on our lives than the actual cash in our wallet, which you will learn much about throughout this book.

There are endless paths to the financial freedom you are seeking, but the two quickest ways are through business and real estate. After observing some of the wealthiest people in the world, Ryan and I noticed a pattern. They all started or inherited a business, and they almost all invested in real estate. We learned to leverage debt instead of avoiding it. I have more debt now than I ever did, but there is one major difference. The debt in real estate is an asset that increases cash flow and my net worth and builds wealth.

For years, I cried so many tears over my guilt of student loan debt. I felt like I was buried in sand and could barely breathe. But it wasn't the actual debt that gave me so much angst; it was the stranglehold I was giving this debt over my life, my value, and my future. It was the beliefs I had around money that I subscribed to for so long. It was the money story I learned and observed as a child that I didn't even know needed to be rewritten. It was the poverty mindset I had grown so comfortable in that I didn't even know how it was affecting my ability to produce more money and abundance in my life.

My hope through this book is that you are expanded, set free, find your own version of financial freedom, divorce your money story, and create a life of abundance for you and the generations to come. It's time to have a breakthrough in your finances and walk into the Kingdom of prosperity God has created for us.

If you are reading this book, you likely aren't where you want to be financially. You have likely tried a million different things. Maybe you've frozen your credit cards (yeah, I've actually done that), maybe you've tried the "cash-in-envelopes" method, you've started a side hustle, you've taken some courses, and even had a garage sale to make some extra cash but year after year you are still seeing the same result in your life. You might feel helpless, frustrated, and overwhelmed when it comes to financial matters, and even talking about your money fills you with anxiety and stress.

You'll find through much of this book that I know those feelings all too well. If I could ask you to do one thing for me while you read through this book, it would be to be open to this process and commit to going all in. It's going to take continual effort to battle your mind, the world, the self-doubt, and the fear. The commitment you make to yourself is the only thing that matters.

It was one book that changed everything for me. It set me on a path to growing more confident in my finances and owning my future. I hope this book does that for you. In order to get where I am now, I had to start by unlearning everything I ever knew about money, success, and wealth.

I'm a self-made multimillionaire who didn't come from money, doesn't have some secret talent that magically multiplies everything I touch, and feels completely unqualified to even write a book about money.

I'm an average girl with average skills, but there's one thing you should know about what I attribute 100% of my success to. I serve a remarkable, limitless, and gracious God who has guided me every step of the way. I didn't sit on my hands and pray God would just change my circumstances with a wave of a magic wand. I took what He gave me and became a steward of the money, time, and talents He placed upon me. While God doesn't promise to make anyone wealthy, God does provide the opportunity for anyone to prosper.

I know it feels impossible and like you are staring down a tunnel with no light at the end. It feels like there's just no way your financial life is going to turn around anytime soon. You doubt if you should even strive for money because even saying, "I want more money," seems selfish and greedy. Sometimes, it feels unfair. You've been faithful, but you just see other people succeeding and wonder, *When will it be my turn?* Financial freedom feels like an empty promise to be realized by only a few of the lucky ones. But that's simply not true, and the journey to financial freedom is so much closer than you think. Let's go on a journey to find what's holding you back, what chains need to be broken, and truly discover what adventure God is calling you to.

Who's ready?

CHAPTER 1

"Poverty Mind" versus "Prosperity Mind"

"Being broke is a state of mind, and living in the poverty spirit is to believe there is no way out."
–Janine Mix

I can remember so vividly being in the line at Starbucks as I was heading to work with a lump in the pit of my stomach. That voice in my head was telling me, *You shouldn't be here. You don't need it. You can't afford it.* I would be in the drive-through riddled with guilt as I placed my order. By the time I got to the window and handed over my money, I thought to myself, *Too late now. You did it. See? You aren't good with money, and you probably never will be.*

It's always the coffee.

For years, I would hear famous rich guys like Dave Ramsey, David Bach, Kevin O'Leary, and hundreds of other (mostly male) financial gurus spout something like, *if you just take the $5 per day that you would've spent on a coffee and invested it instead, you'd be a millionaire by the time you retire.* Anybody else? Like this one expense is the demise of our financial future and the reason we aren't financially savvy.

If you've read the Introduction, you know more about my story. I was living paycheck to paycheck. My life consisted of work, work, eat, work, work, a little sleep, then work some more. It felt miserable. As silly as it sounds, coffee brought me joy, and some days it felt like the only joy I had.

And, here's what that messaging did for me, and maybe you too. The minute the barista handed me my order, my joy instantly turned to remorse. The coffee became an abusive, toxic relationship that constantly reminded me how bad I was with money and how little discipline I had. I beat myself up and went into a spiral of how I shouldn't have bought it, how I never learned my lesson, and sometimes I would even go as far as to punish myself and skip lunch that day. My joy for a simple latte has quickly turned to guilt, shame, and frustration at myself, and now I'll just punish myself by not eating. The thing was, I wasn't putting my coffee on a credit card. I had the money to buy it, but the belief that this coffee was keeping me poor was so ingrained in my mind that I couldn't even enjoy it. I would go back to work discouraged, and each sip felt like a punishment.

But deep down, I realized that none of these rich 'gurus' made their millions by investing their latte money. I would like to see a financial book written by men, for men, which tells them to stop drinking beer and cancel their golf membership. Right, because there isn't a single male that would resonate with that concept—they would see right through it. This was a message directed to women, but where did it come from? It's been around for decades, and I, for one, am sick of hearing it... aren't you?

Now, here is something I want to be crystal clear about. This book and its title aren't a justification to relinquish responsibility for your finances because "you only live once." *Buy the Damn Coffee* is about a movement away from small, incremental, and often insignificant sacrifices to achieve financial success and focusing instead on the bigger transformation of the inner healing of our relationship with money so that you can be a blessing to yourself and others. The title of this book is an anthem for every single woman whose joy in going to her favorite local coffee shop was immediately followed by feelings of regret, guilt, and shame.

And one more important point to remind you: this book is *not* the prosperity gospel. God doesn't promise you wealth, nor is your generosity to your church going to place you in favor with God or have anything to do with your salvation. You can't buy your way to Heaven or bribe your way out of hell. Your money has absolutely nothing to do with your righteousness with God. Now that that's clear, let's uncover what might be holding you back from your true financial potential.

The Poverty Mind

Our world is enslaved to the "Poverty Mind." A belief that there isn't enough to go around and that to live rich is to contribute to the suffering and lack of others. That somehow, your choice to increase your wealth will directly steal from those less fortunate. I see it all over the media, in the judgment of the influencer's comment section, and the ravaging anger of those who think their own lack is the consequence of others who have prospered. The "Poverty Mind" vilifies the rich and believes they should be punished and taken from so that others can have more. The "Poverty Mind" sees the world as a finite piece of pie to be sliced evenly amongst all of humanity and an impossibility of there being another pie once this one is divided.

The "Poverty Mind" is what will scream at volumes so loud you may not want to finish reading this book. It will fool you into believing that wealth and possessions are evil, unnecessary, selfish, and condemned by God.

In this book, I want to share my journey to financial freedom, the challenges and misperceptions around money that tend to hold us back, and how to become a faithful steward of what God provides. I will share how it wasn't skipping my daily latte that finally transformed my life and my finances, and rarely is this the case for some of the wealthiest people today. Coffee is the distraction. It's the small item that keeps you focused on the smaller financial issues that often leave you feeling more broke and enslaved to the "Poverty Mind." The problem with the "latte factor," as some would call it, is that it only focuses on one area of your finances—your expenses—while completely ignoring the other category of your budget, your income.

You can only cut so many expenses from your budget because, eventually, you have a floor. You can't live off of zero, so once you have removed all the discretionary spending from your expenses, you are left with the bare minimum you need to survive. While trimming down your expenses is necessary to correct overspending or prevent you from getting into more debt, this should be seen as a temporary solution to correct a current financial problem. The challenge I see is that many people will stay here for the rest of their lives. They will deprive themselves of spending any money for fear of getting into a bad financial situation.

The oppressive voices of "gurus" continually echo in their heads about how they just need to adjust their spending habits and work harder. And they live in this poverty mindset that tells them they only have this set income, and so the only way to "make more" is by cutting more from their lives. Then, they often resent the life they have built that is now void of date nights, vacations, or coffee.

The next thing that often happens is because they have deprived themselves and worked themselves to the bone, they feel like they have nothing to show for it—not even something as simple as a movie night with their spouse or a weekly indulgence like a coffee is feasible. So, what is the typical behavior that follows that? They'll binge and go on a buying spree to feel less trapped, which often sets them back further financially than before. Therein lies the vicious cycle that keeps so many stuck, broke, and frustrated. There isn't a budget that can break this cycle because it's so much deeper than that.

The true acceleration of your financial life doesn't lie in cutting out your expenses. It's what's on the other side of that budget category that has the greatest potential for long-term change: your income. This income could be from your job, a side hustle, and your investments. Many of you reading this are starting right where I was: at a job, working 40+ hours a week, and feeling like you have nothing left over in your bank account to show for it. You started following the typical financial advice and trimmed away all the extras from your budget, but now you aren't even able to enjoy the money you are making because it's going directly to the bills.

Maybe, like me, you picked up a second job in hopes that you could make some extra cash to pay down your debt faster or have a little fun money to spend on things like eating out with friends or a new pair of shoes. But now you've added an extra 10 hours of work to your week and barely have any time or energy left to hang out with your friends anyway. You want to start saving money, so you've set up an automatic transfer every month to start saving money for emergencies, but then an unexpected bill hits your checking account, and you get the dreaded "insufficient funds" notice as you frantically transfer money back from your savings to your checking to make sure the bill gets paid. Your savings account is drained again. You decide to host a garage sale on the weekend so you can replenish your savings account and pay for the overage you spent this month. You are frustrated and feel like nothing is ever going to change. Each month, you tell yourself, *This is the month I am finally going to get my money in order, start saving, and stop eating out!* But the next month comes, and it's the same story, the same challenges: some random expense comes that you weren't expecting, and eventually "next month" becomes "next year," and five years later, you are still broke, barely have anything saved, and are one emergency away from total financial destruction.

I believe that to be freed from this poverty mindset, you need to adopt a new way of looking at prosperity and stewardship altogether. You must start seeing the world from a glass overflowing instead of half empty. You must see a world full of more pies and a prosperity so full and abundant that God in all His majesty couldn't possibly place us here without everything we need.

The truth is that the "Poverty Mind" is not of God at all. It tricks you into staying stuck and impoverished. It keeps you a prisoner of your circumstances and makes you feel hopeless and helpless.

But how did we get here? To answer that question, we must go back to the beginning.

"On the sixth day of creation, God said, 'Be fruitful and multiply and fill the earth and subdue it, and have dominion over the fish of the sea and over the birds of the heavens and over every living thing that moves on the earth.' And God said, 'Behold, I have given you every living plant yielding seed that is on the face of all the earth, and every tree with seed in its fruit. You shall have them for food. And to every beast of the earth and to every bird of the heavens and to everything that creeps on the earth, everything that has the breath of life, I have given every green plant for food.'" (Genesis 1:28-30).

God planted a lush garden in Eden where rivers flowed, there was gold and onyx, and Adam was put to work to keep it, with one condition.

"And the Lord God commanded the man saying, 'You may surely eat of every tree of the garden, but of the tree of knowledge of good and evil you shall not eat, for in the day that you eat of it you shall surely die.'" (Genesis 2:16-17).

Here, God had just created everything in the entire world, gave Adam a purpose to tend to the garden, allowed him to name all of His creations, and created Eve as a helper fit for him. They both were given dominion over every living thing, and an abundance of food and resources were available for them and every living thing. Surely they had everything they could ever desire because God created in abundance? Well, yes—until the serpent reminded Eve of the one thing they were not to have. The serpent convinced Eve that God was lying: it told her she would not die if she ate from the tree but would instead be like God, knowing good and evil.

"So when the woman saw that the tree was good for food, and it was a delight to the eyes and that the tree was to be desired to make one wise, she took of its fruit and ate, and she also gave some to her husband who was with her, and he ate." (Genesis 3:6).

God gave us everything we needed, and yet we could only focus on the one thing we still lacked. The "Poverty Mind" has been there since the beginning, and as you can see, it didn't come from God.

You start to think this is the way your life is going to be forever. Maybe you want to work for the next 30 years at your job so you can collect retirement benefits from your company. I think a lot of people are content to do so. But maybe, like me, you didn't have any retirement benefits at your job. I had no retirement plan, no savings, and was six figures in debt. I truly believed this was just the hand I had been dealt and that I would be in the constant cycle of living paycheck to paycheck for the rest of my life. To say I know what it's like to live in the "Poverty Mind" would be an understatement. I didn't just know it; I lived it and accepted it as the only way of life I would ever know.

I was frustrated and jealous seeing other people get ahead. I had friends who lived off trust funds and never seemed to have any financial problems. I used to count the amount of money some of my friends were spending weekly on their nails, lashes, clothes, and handbags and was absolutely flabbergasted. That kind of money seemed outrageous and unnecessary. It felt unfair. I was working so hard and wasn't getting anywhere close to that kind of lifestyle. At the time, I couldn't even imagine having that kind of disposable income. Comparison, jealousy, envy: these are all characteristics of the "Poverty Mind."

I was an expert at looking like I had everything together. I was too prideful and worried about what other people would think to let my poverty show. By day, I played a fashionable and successful store manager, but by night, I was eating stale pasta and tomato paste out of the can.

You see, the "Poverty Mind" is quick to judge others. It will make you think that what you wear makes a difference no matter the cost. It will fuel the need to look rich on the outside and fool you into believing that you deserve it. You worked hard. Treat yourself. You only get one life, so YOLO!

There is nothing wrong with treating yourself and enjoying your money. But if it's at the sacrifice of your financial well-being, losing your house to foreclosure, or damaging your credit score, it's never a good idea. I was trying to live a life that my wallet couldn't match up to. I couldn't look past the instant gratification or summon the kind of discipline I needed to correct my financial situation, which I think many of us struggle with. The reason for this isn't because of our need for immediate gratification. It has everything to do with our lack of fulfillment and the dissatisfaction in our lives. Add to this broken budgets that keep you stuck in the expense category, and the "Poverty Mind" anchors us in these beliefs and feelings of hopelessness and causes us to slip further down the path of staying broke.

Don't believe the poverty mindset influences your ability to find financial freedom, build generational wealth, and live a prosperous life full of abundance? Let's play a game.

"Poverty Mind" versus "Prosperity Mind"

Welcome to the show! I'm your host, Janine Mix, and today, I will read a series of statements. As a contestant, you will identify which of these statements is rooted in the "Poverty Mind" and which is rooted in the "Prosperity Mind." Let's start!

Statement: I would rather have happiness than money.
Answer: "Poverty Mind."
The "Prosperity Mind" would say, "I can have both!"

Statement: Look at that expensive bag she has; that seems excessive.
Answer: "Poverty Mind."
The "Prosperity Mind" would say, "What she has doesn't make a difference to me."

Statement: There's enough to provide for my needs and the needs of others.
Answer: "Prosperity Mind."
The "Poverty Mind" would say, "I can't afford to give away money."

Statement: Rich people are arrogant, selfish, and greedy
Answer: "Poverty Mind."
The "Prosperity Mind" would say, "Some might be, but there are plenty of poor people like that, too."

Statement: My money belongs to me. I earned it; it's mine.
Answer: "Poverty Mind."
The "Prosperity Mind" would say, "I am a steward of what God provides."

Statement: There are plenty of resources available to me, including money.
Answer: "Prosperity Mind."
The "Poverty Mind" would say, "There's only so much money in the world."

Statement: If I make more money, it takes from other people.
Answer: "Poverty Mind."
The "Prosperity Mind" would say, "There is no lack or scarcity in the Kingdom."

Statement: Money is a byproduct of creating value for others.
Answer: "Prosperity Mind."
The "Poverty Mind" would say, "I feel bad charging for my services or products."

Identifying where the "Poverty Mind" shows up in your life is critical to understanding your relationship with money, as well as the mental roadblocks that are keeping you stuck and feeling incapable of breaking through. We have to adopt an abundant and prosperous mindset if we are to attempt to change our circumstances once and for all. Someone recently told me that our money identity is the hardest identity to change as we grow in personal development and find healing from our past. Throughout this book, I am going to help you identify your money influencers, understand your behaviors, and help you break free of the "Poverty Mindset" once and for all!

Adopting the "Prosperity Mindset" isn't easy either because when you are struggling financially, it doesn't feel like you are living in a world of abundance. Your bank account doesn't magically overflow on its own. You see yourself and so many other people struggling, which only reinforces this belief that abundance is for the lucky few.

The prosperity perspective shift I had to make that truly accelerated my financial journey was to understand that while expenses have a floor, income has no ceiling. This meant I needed to change *how* I made money. I was living off a finite paycheck, and even a small raise wouldn't be much help.

In the book *Secrets of a Millionaire Mind*, T. Harv Eker states, "Poor people prefer to be paid a steady salary or hourly wage. They need the 'security' of knowing that exactly the same amount of money is coming in at exactly the same time, month in, month out. What they don't realize is that this security comes with a price, and the cost is wealth."

I had just accepted that the only money available to me was the bi-weekly check that I got from my job. I believed that this was all I had to work with, and the only way to make more was to sell more of my time. So I did so, working two jobs from age 8 to 24! I was a master of trading my time for dollars, and for 99% of the population, this is where we all start. When you don't have any money, all you have is your time to sell. When you start making a lot more money, your time becomes your greatest resource, so you either have to charge more for your time, create more value, or buy back time. I chose the security of a job and broke Eker's wealth principle, "Never have a ceiling on your income." The "Poverty Mind" kept me from realizing how much earning potential I had and made me feel there was no way out.

The Prosperity Mind

I've shared a lot about the "Poverty Mind," but what exactly does it mean to have a "Prosperity Mind?"

The "Prosperity Mind" doesn't live in the la-la-land of whimsical fairies, where if you just believe, then all your dreams will come true,, and it doesn't just come in Santa's bag. A prosperous mind is ultimately a shift from a fixed mindset to a growth mindset.

This concept of fixed and growth mindsets was coined by psychologist Carol Dweck in her 2006 book *Mindset: The New Psychology of Success*. Dweck explains that someone with a growth mindset believes they can learn and grow the skills necessary to succeed. They tend to see challenges as a learning opportunity. Someone with a fixed mindset believes they are born with certain skills, knowledge, and abilities that are unable to improve or change. When they fail at a challenge, their fear that they might not succeed often stops them from progressing.

Let's see how this can impact your skills with money. If you are someone who wants to create wealth, you will need to learn financial skills, like how to manage and invest your money to increase your finances. If you have a fixed mindset, you might think, *I've never been that good with money and have no idea where to start when it comes to investing. I'm not smart enough to figure this out or become wealthy.* In contrast, if you approach your money with a growth mindset instead, you might think, *I don't have a background in financial management or investing, but I can learn and grow my skills until I am confident.*

A prosperity mindset goes hand in hand with a growth mindset. It requires you to be open to learning and improving your circumstances through the challenges and obstacles you might face.

Take a look at this chart and try to identify whether you have a fixed mindset or a growth mindset. How do you face challenges and obstacles, and how might your current mindset be helping or harming you? The good news is that you can go from a fixed mindset to a growth mindset.

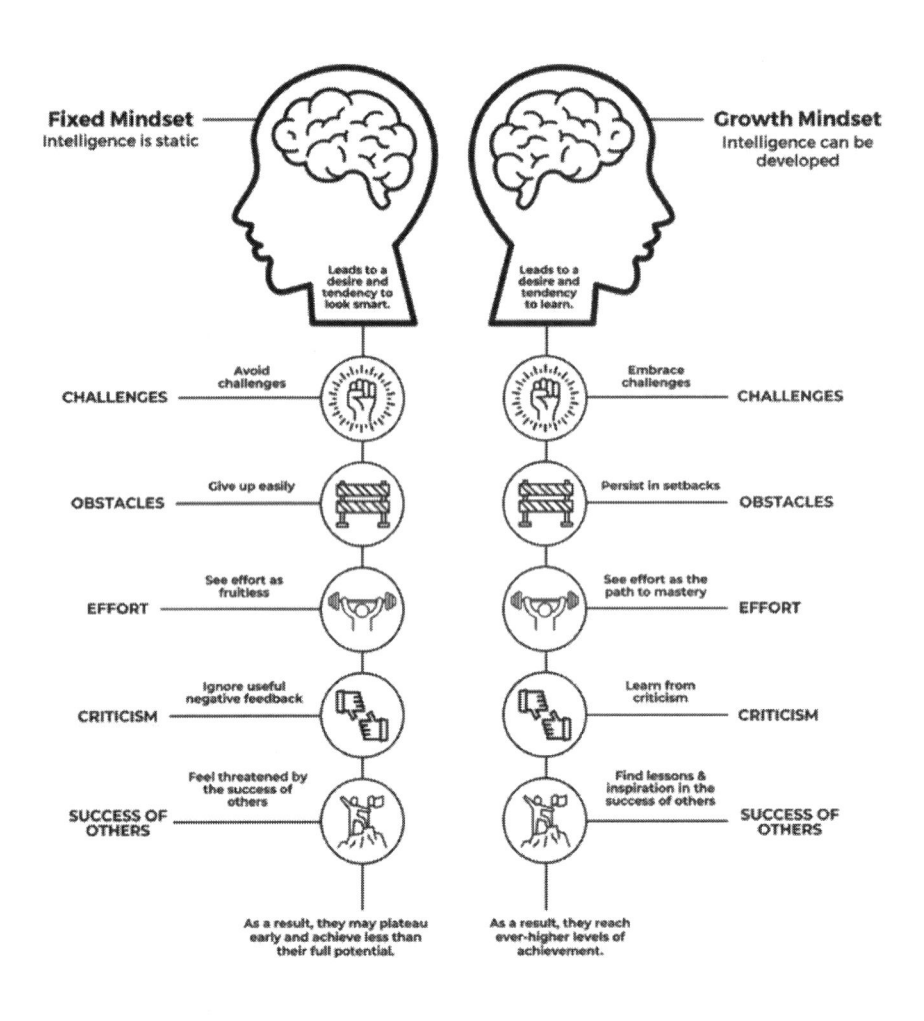

Fixed Mindset — Intelligence is static
Leads to a desire and tendency to look smart.

Growth Mindset — Intelligence can be developed
Leads to a desire and tendency to learn.

	Fixed Mindset	Growth Mindset	
CHALLENGES	Avoid challenges	Embrace challenges	CHALLENGES
OBSTACLES	Give up easily	Persist in setbacks	OBSTACLES
EFFORT	See effort as fruitless	See effort as the path to mastery	EFFORT
CRITICISM	Ignore useful negative feedback	Learn from criticism	CRITICISM
SUCCESS OF OTHERS	Feel threatened by the success of others	Find lessons & inspiration in the success of others	SUCCESS OF OTHERS

As a result, they may plateau early and achieve less than their full potential.

As a result, they reach ever-higher levels of achievement.

When we follow the prosperity mindset, we believe it's possible to change our circumstances. We are filled with the hope and determination to see our goals through. If we do not adopt this mindset, we will fall into the trap of the "Poverty Mind" and accept the hand that was dealt to us, unable to see a pathway out.

So where are you?

Which mindset has driven your thoughts, feelings, and actions?

I was consumed by the poverty mindset. I never thought I was smart enough, talented enough, or would ever have the opportunity to change my circumstances. While working in retail in Los Angeles, I saw people dripping in wealth daily. I would be working with customers like Paris Hilton, Katy Perry, Faith Hill, and so many others, all while remaining unable to pay for my lunch on Beverly Drive.

I started learning about a growth mindset during a time in my life when I was at my absolute lowest. I had just lost my job right before Christmas. My unemployment wasn't much, so I racked up $5,000 worth of debt to help pay for groceries and also make sure my sister and her family had a nice Christmas. I wanted to hide the fact that I was a broke loser "living my dream" in the big city. In reality, I was living in an apartment that was home to hundreds of cockroaches. This is no exaggeration. After I got home from work around 2 a.m. I would prepare myself for the daily battle to take back my territory. I would first set my purse down outside on the porch. Things were about to go down. I quietly turned the key to unlock the door, gently turned the knob, and pushed the door open ever so slowly, just enough to slip my hand through to feel for the light switch. This was it. Once I flipped that switch, I only had a few seconds to catch the enemy off guard.

I would take one deep breath and, with every bit of energy left in me, flip the switch, fling open the door, and start stomping my feet as fast as I could as hundreds of cockroaches scattered back to their hiding places. Once I'd inflicted as much damage as I could, I would check the sticky traps that I had set that morning under all the sinks. They'd invariably be so full you almost couldn't see the bottom. Did you know that a German cockroach lays about 20 to 40 eggs each time? How do I know this? Because when the mother cockroaches would get stuck in the traps, they would lay their eggs. I would come home to new hatches every single night.

This might be disturbing to some of you reading this, but what's more disturbing is that this was the way I lived for nearly six months in this apartment. I lived in a small four-plex. My landlord was also my neighbor, and his entire family of 15 people lived in the three other apartments. They left food out everywhere and had become accustomed to these invaders. When I went to grab a spatula, I would open the kitchen drawer just to see more of them scatter. I stopped eating in my apartment entirely.

Obviously, I had trouble sleeping, knowing they came out at night and were roaming freely. I *never* walked barefoot in my apartment and eventually would shower and couch surf at my friends to try to feel clean. When I was laid off from my job just weeks before Christmas, I was so depressed knowing all I had left was my overpriced cockroach-infested apartment to go home to and stick my head in a pillow and cry.

What a life, huh? I get choked up just thinking about it. I had been working so hard, and just a few months before I was laid off, I was flying around the country, feeling like I had finally made it. It was as if all the years of working at the bottom of the retail food chain were finally paying off. I had my first corporate job, medical benefits, and a corner office on the 25th floor overlooking the ocean on Beverly Drive. Then, 30 days after the company I worked for filed for bankruptcy, I was living off of $900 of unemployment that would expire in three months, wondering what I was going to do next. I watched my nephews and niece each open their brand-new Wii while we listened to Christmas music on my fancy new iPod and speakers, which I had recently financed on my credit card—that I was now paying 20% interest on.

I felt sick to my stomach. I remember how much joy they had and all the memories we made that Christmas, but when they left, my reality set in, and I was so far from where I wanted to be. I fell to my knees and bawled my eyes out. I pleaded with God. What had I done wrong? Why was this happening to me? The "Poverty Mind" swarmed over me and sent me into a depression I didn't think I was going to get out of. It was at that moment that I had another switch turn on, and this time, it didn't require a battle with the cockroaches.

I had this vision that, one day, I would take my nephews and my niece on their first international trip, all-expenses-paid, anywhere they wanted to go. This felt like an impossible dream. I just shared what my reality was. How was I going to afford this? That's the amazing thing about having a growth mindset. In the challenge, you know you are being tested, and there is something you can learn in every circumstance.

You know that God is working for you, not against you. You still have hope that things can and will change. The "Prosperity Mind" can be stubborn if you let it. It will start to motivate you in impossible ways. I'm not going to tell you that this was an overnight process by any means. But the growth mindset can change your perspective on life so you can move forward towards that reality by shifting your mindset from, *Life is always going to be this way for me,* to *What would I need to change in my life to make this a reality?*

The timing of life is never what you expect it to be, but somehow, God's timing is always better. Nearly ten years later, I was sitting next to my oldest nephew, who had just turned 18, on a 10-hour flight to a two-week, all-expenses paid trip to New Zealand, laughing hysterically at literally nothing because we were so sleep-deprived. I had so many tears of gratitude on that trip.

A few years later, we took his brother to Madeira, Portugal, and just last year, we took the youngest on her trip to Iceland. I fulfilled the vision I had over ten years ago and the promise to myself that I would change my circumstances. I thought this crazy idea that I came up with in the absolute worst financial moment of my life would change their lives. What I didn't realize was that this big, scary, impossible dream would actually change mine. It was this dream that kept me motivated. Every time the "Poverty Mind" crept in and told me I couldn't do it or that it would never happen, the

"Prosperity Mind" kept me inspired and dreaming about the memories we would make. Every time something unexpected came up that would set me back again, the "Poverty Mind" would remind me how far away I was. It was the prosperity mindset that kept me moving forward through all the highs and lows. It wasn't some manifestation; it was simply the belief that God had bigger plans for me and wasn't done with me yet. It was my faith that kept me focused, my stewardship that would be rewarded, and my "Prosperity Mind" that propelled me forward.

Wherever you are in life right now, you can change your circumstances. I'm proof, and there are so many inspiring stories of others who have, too.

You will be tried and tested through the fire, but your current circumstances and past do not define your life; they will simply refine you.

The "Prosperity Mind" is filled with hope, growth, and a path forward.

"'For I know the plans I have for you,' declares the Lord, 'plans to prosper you and not to harm you, plans to give you hope and a future.'" (Jeremiah 29:11).

This is a part of God's plan, too. He doesn't give you the promise of wealth, but He does give you the opportunities to prosper in all areas of your life. Don't let the "Poverty Mind" tell you otherwise.

CHAPTER 2

Common Money Myths

"Money is only a tool. It will take you wherever you wish, but it will not replace you as the driver."
–Ayn Rand

Have you ever seen the show *MythBusters,* where hosts Adam Savage and Jamie Hyneman spend an entire episode scientifically proving or disproving some of the greatest myths, folklore, and internet videos of all time? They cover everything from what happens when you mix soda with Mentos to whether duct tape actually fixes anything. One of the most popular episodes they did was recreating Frank Morris and the Anglin Brothers escaping from Alcatraz using an inflatable raft made from rubber raincoats. Was the escape actually possible, and could they have survived? It was an entertaining, eye-opening show, with 15 seasons of mind-blowing discoveries, all in pursuit of proving or disproving common myths. That is what I am setting out to do in this chapter of the book because, like *MythBusters,* there are some very common money myths that have circulated for generations.

In my years of studying the subject of money and coaching hundreds of entrepreneurs through their businesses, I found that there are essentially four common money myths that plague our minds and bleed into our subconscious.

Myth #1: Money Is Evil

There are hundreds of Bible verses that talk about money:

- *"Do not lay up for yourselves treasures on earth, where moth and rust destroy and where thieves break in and steal [...] For where your treasure is, there your heart will be also." (Matthew 6:19-21)*
- *"It is easier for a camel to go through the eye of a needle than a rich person to enter the kingdom of God." (Mark 10:25)*
- *"No one can serve two masters, for either he will hate the one and love the other, or he will be devoted to the one and despise the other. You cannot serve God and money" (Matthew 6:24)*

When you take some of these verses at face value, money doesn't seem that great.

Then you look at Hollywood and see all kinds of movies and TV shows with bank robbers, drug dealers, scam artists, gamblers, conmen, and every other kind of heartless, ruthless antagonist pursuing the same thing: money.

And if you are living with a Poverty Mind, as I mentioned in the last chapter, you might already view money as a scarce resource. After all, if everyone on Earth is just sharing one finite money pie, the ones who have an abundance of it seem to be hoarding from those who need it. Are all rich people greedy, or does money corrupt them? Either way, it's wrong.

You rarely hear about money at church. You don't learn about money in school. And the only thing you heard about money at home was how your dad hates his job because he's working long hours for little pay while his boss leaves at noon every day to play golf. But if the kids want to eat, Dad has to work.

Yeah, money sucks.

Well, here's the honest truth. Money is not inherently evil or good. Those who believe it to be evil likely haven't been around a lot of generous wealthy people, have watched way too many documentaries on Netflix about greed and corruption, or have misinterpreted scripture.

But wait, doesn't God say that money is the root of all evil and that the poor are blessed and will inherit the Kingdom of God?

Well, actually, most verses about money are often misquoted or misunderstood, and many of these subjects simply come down to where our hearts lie. Money is not the root of all evil, and here's where this myth is easily busted.

"For the love of money is a root of all kinds of evil" (1 Timothy 6:10)

It's not an emphasis on money; it's an emphasis on the love of money.

This is where you see greed and corruption enter the heart, and you see money being used for illicit industries, like the drug trade (a 300-billion-dollar industry) and human trafficking (a 130-billion-dollar industry). Money isn't the cause behind this evil; sin is.

Money is just a tool. You can use this tool to pay your bills, buy a new car, put food on your table, provide a roof over your head, donate to your church, and bless others. But just like any tool, if used incorrectly, it can cause a lot of harm.

A hammer is also a tool. It can be used to build a bookshelf, hang a painting, or kill someone. When you go to jail for killing someone, the jury doesn't convict the tool of this cruel and deadly crime. They convict the person who was holding the tool. They look at motive, evidence, and witnesses, all to establish whether the person holding the hammer committed a crime. The hammer didn't have any ill intent, and no one will testify on the stand that it was the hammer's fault for being a dangerous tool. It has no merit or blame on its own until it is used outside of what it was made for. Like the hammer, money is also a tool. It can be used for many purposes. It's the intent of the person with this tool, and what they do with it that will be judged.

Somewhere along the way, maybe unintentionally, an idea developed in our church communities that money is a bad thing and to desire it is wrong. We hear verses like Matthew 6:24, *"No one can serve two masters. Either you will hate the one and love the other, or you will be devoted to the one and despise the other. You cannot serve both God and money."* From this, we determine that if we have to choose money or God, we will obviously choose God. So, if God is good, money must be wrong. Was God saying to avoid money at all costs?

Of course not. Throughout scripture, God is teaching us that we can't earn or buy our way into Heaven. God reminds us that we can't take our Earthly possessions with us, so we should not love the world or desire things of the flesh. He teaches us to remain focused on Him. He uses parables and stories to help us understand the issues of the heart. When it comes to money, as believers, we are to manage our resources wisely, give praise to our God who provides, and serve Him with it. This does not mean to avoid money or that money is evil. It's simply a matter of the heart.

If money is so bad, why would God instruct the Israelites to plunder the Egyptians as Moses was leading them out of captivity? They took silver, gold, and jewels and made off with an absolute fortune, even though they were heading out into the desert where they couldn't use any of it!

If money is so bad, why was the Tabernacle made out of the finest gold, wood, and materials, and probably cost an obscene amount of money to construct? Why wouldn't God be OK with some basic drywall and two-by-fours from Home Depot?

If money is so bad, why would God have given it to Solomon or Job? The Bible explicitly tells us that God made these two figures insanely rich. Scholars believe that both of these men could've been the richest men in the world during their times, and it's still believed that Solomon was the richest man to ever live and who will ever live.

If money is so bad, why are charities always throwing fundraisers? Or why do churches take an offering?

Throughout the Bible, God repeatedly calls us to be good money managers. A good manager is one who knows how to protect, multiply, and prudently handle something they've been entrusted with. Take the parable of the talents, for example. A talent is a denomination of money that would be equivalent to about a million dollars today. Not just a few coins. A million dollars!

The Parable of the Talents (Also translated as "Bags of Gold")

"Again, it will be like a man going on a journey who called his servants and entrusted his wealth to them. To one he gave five bags of gold, to another two bags, and to another one bag, each according to his ability. Then he went on his journey. The man who had received five bags of gold went at once and put his money to work and gained five bags more. So also, the one with two bags of gold gained two more. But the man who had received one bag went off, dug a hole in the ground, and hid his master's money.

After a long time, the master of those servants returned and settled accounts with them. The man who had received five bags of gold brought the other five. 'Master,' he said, 'you entrusted me with five bags of gold. See, I have gained five more.'

His master replied, 'Well done, good and faithful servant! You have been faithful with a few things; I will put you in charge of many things. Come and share your master's happiness!'

The man with two bags of gold also came. 'Master,' he said, 'you entrusted me with two bags of gold; see, I have gained two more.'

His master replied, 'Well done, good and faithful servant! You have been faithful with a few things; I will put you in charge of many things. Come and share your master's happiness!'

Then, the man who had received one bag of gold came. 'Master,' he said, 'I knew that you are a hard man, harvesting where you have not sown and gathering where you have not scattered seed. So I was afraid and went out and hid your gold in the ground. See, here is what belongs to you.'

His master replied, 'You wicked, lazy servant! So you knew that I harvest where I have not sown and gather where I have not scattered seed? Well then, you should have put my money on deposit with the bankers so that when I returned, I would have received it back with interest.'

'So take the bag of gold from him and give it to the one who has 10 bags. For whoever has will be given more, and they will have an abundance. Whoever does not have, even what they have, will be taken from them. And throw that worthless servant outside, into the darkness, where there will be weeping and gnashing of teeth.'" (Matthew 25:14–30).

There are several lessons we can glean from this parable. First of all, the master separated them by their skills. Right away, he didn't have a lot of confidence in the servant to whom he gave one talent. To the other servants, he gave multiple. *They were given what he felt they could manage.*

The second thing we can learn is *he rewarded the ones who multiplied what they were given.* Stewardship is so much more than organizing the money you have. In the case of these servants, good stewardship required multiplication of what they had. For where you multiply, more can be given and entrusted, as seen in this example. The two servants who multiplied their talents were doubled the reward, and the one who stored instead of stewarded was cursed.

We can also learn from this to do well with what we have, whether it's $10 or $10,000. All three were given the same opportunity to steward what they were given. It didn't matter that one was given more than the other. What mattered was the stewardship of what they were personally given.

So the big question to ask, and what we can learn from this parable, is: what am I doing with what God has given?

Maybe like I used to be, your hands are clenched closed, and your fists are tight. You are holding onto what you have with all your might. The struggle with this approach is that it not only stops you from opening your palms to receive more, but it also limits how much you can fit in your hands.

Maybe, like the last servant, you've stored up and saved some money. You've done the responsible thing and might be sitting on a small nest egg, but you're still wondering when God is going to multiply it. Here's your reality check: it's not God's responsibility to do something with it. It's yours.

Think of money like an electric current (today, money is literally called "currency"). The energy of that current needs to flow continuously for there to be light and for the power to be kept on. Money is also a form of energy, and that energy needs to move through you, not stop at you.

I believe that all money belongs to God.

Every talent, every skill, every dollar that is available in this world belongs to the provider of it all. But He's also provided us with skills, talents, abilities, and experiences that have made us more like Him and shaped our characters more closely into alignment with Him. And we don't serve a limitless and stingy God. We don't serve a God that questions any amount of provisions. We don't serve a God whose glass is half empty or who only has one pie. We serve a God who's flowing in abundance. And the one thing He asked us to do is to test Him with our faithfulness, our money, our finances, and what He is calling us to do in that stewardship. And I, for one, am here for the test. I want to be the best steward of the resources that God entrusts to me, especially money, so that I can make more income and more impact, and I'm thinking if you are reading this book, you do too.

Myth #2: Debt is Bad

Here's a story about a kid who was born into poverty. He had a speech impediment so severe that he couldn't even pronounce his name. His family suffered through the Great Depression, where he learned to make money selling Cokes and newspapers. Then World War II came, and he and his brother got drafted into the Army. He was at war for three years before being honorably discharged.

After getting back home from the Army, he and his brother decided to start a small restaurant. They pooled together what little money they had and borrowed another $6,600, the equivalent of over $100,000 in today's money. In other words, they went into debt.

Their restaurant concept was a 24-hour diner. It was successful, but it was hard work. He and his brother each worked alternating 12-hour shifts, and there were times that he remembers not sitting down for 36 hours straight. He was a single man at the time, and this business was his baby. It had to succeed. It was all they had.

Then, his brother suddenly died in a tragic accident, leaving him to run the diner by himself. His brother's widow tried to help, but she found it too difficult. So, she sold her interest to the young entrepreneur, allowing him to continue all on his own.

He tried to grow by opening a second location, spreading himself even thinner. But that restaurant ended up catching on fire and completely burned to the ground. He was at a turning point. He couldn't keep doing what he was doing. It was too hard, and it wasn't working. He had to do something different.

After some brainstorming, he noticed an item on his menu that was selling really well. That was it! He decided to go all in on his top seller and start a franchise restaurant.

Forty-five years later, this top-selling menu item turned him into a billionaire. The company he created has experienced 52 years of consecutive sales growth, operates over 2,900 locations, and now generates $11 billion in revenue a year. On a sales-per-store basis, it generates more than Burger King, Kentucky Fried Chicken, Domino's, and Subway combined. And the most amazing part is that all 2,900+ locations nationwide aren't even open on Sundays.

This entrepreneur is Truett Cathy, and his company is Chick-fil-A. His company now continues to scale debt-free, but if it weren't for that original loan he and his brother used to start their first restaurant, the Dwarf House, he wouldn't have had the resources to start.

Since its founding, the company has donated over $68 million dollars to charities and educational programs, all because two brothers decided to take a risk, start a business, and leverage debt to help them get started. Think about how many lives they have changed: the employees provided with income, franchise owners who found financial freedom in partnering with this business, and the countless people who have come to know Jesus through the hearts and mission of this one company. I would say this is an incredible example of ministry in the marketplace and being stewards of what God has given them.

I've heard countless times that debt is bad and you should get out of it and avoid it at all costs. However, it's probably safe to say that if it weren't for Truett Cathy's strategic use of debt, Chick-fil-A would not be here today. The positive impact that Chick-fil-A has had on society is immeasurable. But did it all start because of a misdeed? Is debt still bad? Was Truett right to use someone else's money to start his first restaurant, or should he have waited until he had enough of his own?

There is no financial topic that has been forced down the throats of Christians more relentlessly than the topic of debt. We've been scared, intimidated, and called stupid for having it. It's suggested that our highest moral obligation is to get out of it. But is this true?

Before we dive further into the topic of debt, I have to set one thing straight. I despise the words "good" debt and "bad" debt. I think we as a society should collectively work together to change this narrative because there is one absolute truth about debt: it is incoherent to consider it in terms of morality or the absence thereof.

Debt is not a moral construct. Debt has no feelings and is neither good nor bad. The same can be said about money in general, not just debt. Kind of like that tool analogy I mentioned in the last myth. A tool—like a hammer, or a potato peeler, or a paintbrush—isn't innately good or bad. It's just a tool with no feelings or morality.

How you *feel* about debt is an entirely different conversation, though. When I was in $120,000 of student loan debt, I felt handcuffed to the bank, like I wouldn't be able to breathe until it was paid off. I honestly felt I was locked into a contract with evil companies who just wanted me to suffer. They didn't care that I was struggling to make the payments, sleeping in my car, and crying every day. In fact, I believed with every fiber in my body that banks were evil. At one point, the bank needed my father's signature on an updated document.

At the time, my father was at home in hospice because he was diagnosed with terminal cancer. My mother had power of attorney for my dad and signed the paperwork because he was in and out of consciousness while on pain medicine. I emailed over the paperwork, and the bank called and told me they would not accept my mother's signature. I explained the delicacy of the situation to the support representative over the phone, only to be followed with, "It's not my problem. We need your father's signature to proceed." I was bawling my eyes out and filled with so much anger at this woman. How greedy and heartless this bank must be to not even care. My dad was quite literally on his deathbed. We actually had to take him off his IV drip of pain meds and wait a few days so we could lift him up, place a pen in his hand, and make sure he was alert enough to sign it.

Gosh, that's painful to even recall. I just remember my mom and I crying and telling my dad we were sorry we had to do this. And while, yeah, it seems like this representative could have done something different for us, she was just an employee trying to do her job. Back then, I thought she was a heartless, horrible person and never wanted to bank with this company again. I felt like a victim. Just a number in their system. While my reality at the time was completely wrapped in the emotions debt and the banks made me feel, the simple fact was that I had borrowed money to get a degree I couldn't afford. I used someone else's money to get my four-year education, and when I graduated, I would need to start paying back the money I borrowed. When I put it that way, it isn't emotional at all.

But then I would hear all these experts talk about getting out of debt as soon as possible, and what a moron I was to even get myself into this position in the first place. Was that true? Was I just an idiot? Well, you tell me which of the following are dumber. On the one hand, there's persuading an 18-year-old to sign off on $120,000 worth of debt when she has never even opened up a credit card, convincing her that the only way to get a high-paying job in the future is to go to college, where her general educational classes consisted of biology and two years of a foreign language, but not a single class on finances and investing. On the other hand, there's shaming her later in life for having debt, even though this was the path she was convinced would be the only way to succeed.

When you look back at this belief of debt being wrong, you can basically trace it back to one major influencer, Dave Ramsey. Is he the only person who ever said that? No. But he is definitely the loudest. For the last 30 years, he has perpetuated the idea that *all* debt is bad, dangerous, and harmful, and you should avoid it at all costs.

He tells us we need to get three jobs, sell our cars, eat rice and beans, and sacrifice our entire lives to pay our debt off. But why? Dave is notorious for his phrase, "If you will live like no one else today, later you can live like no one else." I don't know about you, but I'm not willing to live on rice and beans in the hopes that I will be able to live a full and abundant life later. I'm not promised tomorrow. And just eliminating my debt payments doesn't automatically mean my life is going to be full and abundant, either! I don't want to starve myself by eating rice and beans, do you? All because he and a few other anti-debt, "stop-buying-coffee," financial gurus tell us this is the path to financial freedom? Who decided that? I know a lot of debt-free, broke people. Sure, they don't have any debt, but that still doesn't mean they are financially free.

I personally know tons of people who have followed his seven baby steps to get out of debt and are now more scared to enjoy money and invest than before. They have been paralyzed in Poverty Mind. Dave Ramsey is brilliant at marketing and business. You think he's worth $300,000,000—read that again: *three hundred million* dollars—because he lives off rice and beans, sold his cars, and doesn't go to Starbucks? Not only does he have an extremely successful business, but he also owns over $600,000,000 in debt-free real estate. I repeat: he didn't get the money to pay for all that real estate because he built up enough cash in his miscellaneous envelope. Are you hearing me?

I'm not condoning spending money you don't have on something you don't need and don't know how you'll repay. Dave and I can agree that's stupid. Where we disagree is that I don't think *you're* stupid.

You do have to build good financial habits and heal your relationship with money. There will be a time of temporary sacrifice if you are going to fix a current harmful financial situation, but this does not need to be a lifelong stranglehold. Only you can define what financial freedom means to you. Everyone's version of financial freedom is specific to themselves. In many cases, our versions of financial freedom are defined by someone else's definition, which might not even align with what we want in our lives.

For some people, financial freedom is being debt-free. For others, it's having enough money to save, invest, and have enough left over to enjoy for themselves and their family. For people like Robert Kiyosaki, wealth and financial freedom are measured in time, not money. According to Kiyosaki, you become financially free when your passive income surpasses your expenses. This is the route I have chosen to find my version of financial freedom. I've acquired enough rental properties that produce passive income to pay my bills, fund my lifestyle, and buy back my time.

And don't even get me started about what I learned about debt from my church. Anytime I would hear sermons at church referring to Proverbs 22:7, *"The rich rules over the poor, and the borrower is a slave of the lender,"* I would feel even worse. I felt that because I had debt, I must have been sinning. It's against God's will, so I have obviously done something wrong. Of course, I didn't realize that this verse was simply an observation of debt bondage - an ancient practice of literal slavery. The preacher never mentioned that. I just assumed it meant I was a disappointment.

My husband Ryan wrote an entire chapter on this topic in his book *Bible Money Secrets: Revealing the Surprising Truths on Debt, Wealth, and Riches*. In the book, he says, "The uses of debt are as varied as the uses for knives—you can use a knife to murder someone, but you can also use it to prepare a salad. Surely, not all uses of debt are biblically condemned."

After interviewing various theologians and doing lots of research for his book, his findings were that there is simply no scripture, indirect readings, or a compilation of various nuances in scripture that say debt is sinful and/or borrowing is sinful.

This is a very important discovery in our money myth-busting, so don't let it slip by or say to yourself, *Well, I guess that's true, but I still need my debt paid off before I can do anything else.* While this may be true depending on your financial situation and goals, the point I am trying to make here is to make wise decisions around your debt, not emotional ones. When we say good or bad debt, we are automatically giving debt a permission slip into our emotions and responses.

The reason Dave Ramsey built his entire business around getting out of debt was because, early on in his life, he started investing in real estate, and he got burned. Foreclosure and bankruptcy took everything from him. He had what I call a "money event" (more on that in the upcoming chapter). This event was so pivotal that it would shape the next 30+ years of his life: he would avoid debt forever and mentor millions of people to do the same.

Ah, there it is. Could it be that the reason we think debt is bad is because one brilliant businessman has been influencing us through the tough, emotional experience he had with it once? But just because something burns you once doesn't mean you have to avoid it forever. Viewing *all* debt as bad is simply not true, nor is it a sound approach to making financial decisions.

While Dave's overall message of financial responsibility is good, his emotional approach surrounding debt has sadly stunted the growth and understanding of countless people who could've otherwise experienced more opportunities and less stress had they simply learned a healthier viewpoint. It's like eliminating hammers from your life because you banged your thumb once. You're just imposing fears and limitations on yourself that are completely unhelpful and restrictive.

The moment you let go of how your debt makes you feel and the stranglehold it has over you is the moment you can start to take back your life. This is the place where you get clarity and can create a plan that includes your mental and physical well-being.

Don't get me wrong here. That doesn't mean you should just rack up credit card bills and be irresponsible with money. Freeing yourself of the shame and guilt around your debt opens the door to learning and understanding that there are different types of debt. There are also multiple strategies for paying off debt that don't include cutting out everything that is fun or enjoyable. When you come out of this emotional debt fog, you can really understand how money works and eventually use debt as a tool to grow your business or investments.

Being debt-free might be a great goal for you. Of course, Ryan and I personally work toward paying off some of our rental properties to increase cash flow, or our car loans, and eventually paid off my student loans. We simply didn't make this the *only* goal. Like I said before, I've known a lot of people who are solely focused on becoming debt-free, but then what? Many of those people devote everything to paying off their debt but then realize they still have bills, they still have to work at their job, they still have to ask for time off, and they still rely solely on their company 401(k) for their retirement. What would happen if they lost their job? What do they do if they only want to work a few days a week? Are they really free?

We have leveraged our rental properties to generate more money and wealth using other people's money (aka debt). This is the #1 strategy we used to build up our multimillion-dollar real estate business and the strategy that most successful investors use too. I'm not going to be shy here because that's not going to benefit anyone, but we have used debt to make us so much more than the interest we have paid. We also used assets to pay off liabilities faster than we could have done by cutting coffee.

For example, in one of the first real estate properties we bought, I was able to pay off $80,000 of my student loans in three years. Yeah, we used one debt to pay off another. Not only did I pay this off faster than I could have using the traditional snowball method, but now we have a cash-flowing asset that has paid us on time every month for the last 12 years. And we still enjoyed our coffees and vacations in the process!

If you have a bunch of money sitting in a savings account, especially with the current inflation rates (7.1% as of writing this book), the truth is you're losing money. If you want to get in the game of money and build wealth faster, you can't just rely on your own small resources. You might need to leverage money and borrow from someone else for a period of time. It doesn't need to be emotional. You're just using a tool. That's all. To even begin to use debt, you have to understand that not all debt is created equal.

Instead of "good" debt, we call this "leverage" debt.

Instead of "bad" debt, we call this "consumer" debt.

The difference is simple: one puts money in your pocket, and one takes money out.

It's not my place to tell anyone that they should or shouldn't have debt. It's also just bad advice to tell you that *all* debt is created equal and that you should simply avoid it. The message I want to share is to learn about debt and the many ways you can use it to invest, start a business, and grow. Learning about debt instead of fearing it changed my life.

So, now you know the debt isn't bad, doesn't have feelings, and isn't a sin; I think it's safe to say this myth is *busted*!

Myth #3: Rich People Are Greedy

A good movie usually involves a character or story with a deep desire for something. This is why it's no surprise that greed is one of the main themes in some of the most influential films of all time. Greed is one of the most intense and selfish desires, therefore making it a solid plot for a villain in the next Hollywood blockbuster.

There Will Be Blood focuses on a silver miner turned oilman who goes on a quest for massive wealth in Southern California's oil boom in the late 19th century. It's here that Daniel Plainview established an oil company and embarked on a career of deceit, coercion, and manipulation that culminates in his killing a member of a family whose land he purchased the right to mine. The man comes to him seeking compensation, feeling the family was cheated, and the protagonist beats him to death with a bowling pin. In a notable monologue, he says, "I have a competition in me. I want no one else to succeed. I hate most people. There are times when I look at people and see nothing worth liking. I want to earn enough money that I can get away from everyone."

The Godfather is a mob drama focusing on a powerful Italian-American crime family with violence, betrayal, and illegal family business.

In *The Wolf of Wall Street*, Jordan Belfort makes his fortune by defrauding wealthy investors out of millions. Sex, drugs, thrills—all for wealth and power.

In *Scarface*, Tony Montana becomes the biggest drug lord in Miami, fighting a war with the Colombian drug cartel and losing his battle with his own drug-induced paranoia.

But it's not all Wall Street and drug plots that emphasize greed. Even Christmas classics like *The Grinch* highlight issues of the heart, as the Grinch tries to steal Christmas and holiday cheer from Whoville. Or what about Disney's classic *The Lion King*, where Scar is so filled with greed and jealousy that he sends Simba, the heir to the throne, into a deadly stampede in an attempt to kill him? When Scar has the chance to save his brother Mufasa, he takes this opportunity to send him plummeting to his death in order to rule the land once and for all.

I hope you are catching on here. Do you think it's possible our views of greed have been widely shaped by programming on the television and plots in the movies?

We become so quick to judge others and their hearts when we see them in positions of power and authority. To be honest, I think this is more out of jealousy and insecurity than anything else. Of course, there are greedy people in the world, but how does that personally affect your desire for wealth?

Money doesn't change you; it just magnifies who you already are.

Chances are, if you are reading this and concerned about becoming greedy, you aren't a greedy person to start with. Think about it: greedy people aren't worried about being greedy. They *are* greedy. They don't care about anyone else, and they run in a totally different, selfish state of mind. This is an issue of the heart, not the cash in their bank account.

My husband and I were once in a Bible study group. Another couple who attended had started a business, and it was doing really well. When we went around asking what we could pray for, this guy asked that we pray for his company because he was worried it was doing so well. Ryan and I were both so confused. We wondered, *What's the problem?*

Well, the problem wasn't that his business was doing well, and he was afraid he would embezzle it or gamble it away. The real problem was that he didn't feel worthy of it, and somewhere along the way, he learned that money is a bad thing. For the reasons discussed above, Christians tend to revere poverty as virtuous and riches as dishonorable. The Bible doesn't explicitly say being rich or wealthy is a bad thing, nor does it characterize poverty as holy or moral. Let me explain.

God doesn't say the poor are blessed; He says in Matthew 5:3, *"Blessed are the poor in spirit, for they will inherit the kingdom of God."* The poor in spirit are talking about their own spiritual lack before God. It has no connection to financial poverty.

In Matthew 19:24, Jesus said to his disciples, *"Truly I tell you, it is hard for a rich man to enter the kingdom of heaven. Again I tell you, it is easier for a camel to pass through the eye of a needle than for a rich man to enter the kingdom of God."*

Here's where understanding context and culture is important. Jesus wasn't saying that rich people are greedy and going to have a harder time getting to Heaven. What Jesus is teaching us is that it's impossible for anyone to be saved on his own merits. At that time, wealth was seen as proof of God's approval. What was often taught by the rabbis was that since rich people had wealth, they were blessed by God and, therefore, would be the most likely candidates for Heaven. Jesus is destroying that notion, along with the idea that anyone can earn eternal life. Salvation has nothing to do with earning it by becoming a wealthy and generous person. *"We are saved through God's grace, mercy, and faith"* (Ephesians 2:8-9). We can't buy salvation.

I told you the story of Truett Cathy earlier. He was rich. Was he greedy? Billy Graham was worth $25 million when he died. Was he greedy? Tim Tebow is rich. It's estimated he's worth around $70 million, and he has been able to do incredible things for people through the Tim Tebow Foundation—with money. In contrast, I know a lot of poor, greedy people, too.

We once had a tenant who flushed rocks down his toilet to make it seem like we were neglectful landlords. His aim was to convince the eviction judge not to evict him immediately, allowing him to continue living rent-free for a longer period. That was greedy. We had another tenant who would go from church to church looking for help to pay rent. Every time she would get behind she would find another generous and helpful congregation. Soon enough, our building was getting new paint and a few months of paid-up rent. It took the third church to call us before we realized she was taking advantage of them and prying on the goodwill of these people. We kindly declined the church's money.

By the time she was being evicted, she started taking advantage of her own grandmother, who was living with her. She stole money and left her grandmother homeless to figure it out on her own. It was terribly selfish and greedy. You see, it's not someone's money that makes them greedy or generous.

My prayer for you is that you release these fears of greed and instead seek God's wisdom around money and stewardship. Don't compare your riches to another, and don't fall into spiritual poverty for the sake of your accomplishments and contentment with yourself and your wealth. The opposite of greed is *generosity*. Make this a main practice in your wealth building, and honor God through your faithfulness.

Money is the only topic on which God asks us to test Him, so maybe it's time to put that myth to the test.

Myth #4: Money Doesn't Buy You Happiness

If you are living comfortably with two cars in the garage, Christmas presents for your kids, the latest gadget in your pocket, and a standing brunch date with your besties every weekend, chances are, yes, more money won't buy you more happiness. A Princeton University study found that there is a law of diminishing returns when your income rises above $75,000-ish.[1] Once our basic needs are met, consumerism and more stuff won't make us happier. Sometimes, it can actually have the opposite effect.

And when we are told that money can't buy us happiness, it's usually by some well-dressed, well-fed, and well-rested individual who had a warm shower and a convenient breakfast that morning. But if you're reading this from your sunlit reading nook, here's what's important to realize. 99% of the world is poorer than you. A lot poorer.

And while it's technically true that money can't purchase happiness, it can remove a lot of pain. I spent most of my early years in life suffering simply because I didn't have money to help me solve problems.

The nights I would sleep in my car so I wouldn't get another parking ticket could have been solved if I simply had the money to buy a monthly pass in the parking garage across the street.

I broke down in tears at a doctor's office simply because I couldn't afford the copay to be seen. I lived with chronic pain for years because I couldn't afford the treatment I needed. It was agonizing.

I remember getting hit with a huge, unexpected $800 phone bill once. For you youngins out there, this was back in the day when you didn't have unlimited minutes, and if you were outside of the distance of certain cell towers, they would charge you extra for "roaming." When I opened this bill, I felt my heart sink, like I got punched in the stomach. It was a devastating blow and about half of my regular paycheck. I had no idea how I was going to pay it. I called the phone company and pleaded with them, admitting that I had no idea I was outside of my network, and I begged them to remove the charges. They didn't budge.

At the time, I had a two-hour commute to work, so I would tune into KIIS FM with Ryan Seacrest. There was a series they started where Seacrest would pay your bills. You could submit any bill, and he would call out names every morning on the radio. Once your name was called, you had 30 minutes to call the station back, and they would put you on air and pay your bill. It was a clever campaign to retain listeners, and it was my only hope. I faxed in my bill along with a letter of desperation (if you don't know what a fax is, ask your parents). I would spend hours listening in the morning on my commute, praying to hear my name. If I was scheduled to work, I would ask my friends and family to tune in so they could let me know if they heard my name. This was also pre-smartphone days, so you couldn't just listen in on an app. You had to log into their website or have a radio nearby.

I spent more time with KIIS FM than I want to admit. I was glued to the station with a heart full of hope and my fingers crossed. The weeks passed by, and I would send my bill via fax every few days. I spent hours and hours tuning into the station, and just as I was losing all hope and the due date was approaching, I heard, "Janine Fry, Ryan would like to pay your bill!" I panicked. I pulled off the road and started dialing. I was shaking. Was I delusional? Did he actually say my name? What if I can't get connected? I dialed in. Busy. I tried again. Busy. It must have been only a few short minutes, but it felt like an eternity before I got through.

"Hello, this is Janine Fry. My name was just called."

"Ok, please hold, and we will put you through."

My heart was beating so hard I thought I was going to pass out. I got on-air and Ryan Seacrest said, "Hello, Janine, we would like to pay your phone bill."

I screamed with joy, and tears ran down my face. I thanked him so much and kept yelling, "Ryan Seacrest paid my bill!" After I got off the air and gave them the details, I started getting calls from all the friends and family members who were doing their part in helping me and had heard me on the radio. It was a moment I will never forget and a blessing at the last hour. The amount of lost time, agony, and stress I experienced over this one bill simply wouldn't have happened if I had the money to pay it.

I know my story isn't unique. I know there are many people out there experiencing similar circumstances. Unable to pay rent, being evicted, losing a job, stuck riding the bus because their car broke down, and unable to get a gift for their child's birthday. These issues simply wouldn't be issues if they had money.

In a survey by Empower, more than half of Americans (59%) say money *can* buy happiness. Some 71% believe more money would solve most of their problems, and a third of them said a relatively attainable amount of $15,000 would make a meaningful impact on their lives. Their data showed that "Return on Happiness" (ROH) isn't about reaching some far-out net worth;

it's achieved by addressing money milestones like being able to pay bills on time, living debt-free, affording everyday luxuries without worry, and owning a home.[2]

I bet there's something in your life right now that's causing you stress, anxiety, or harm. How would an extra $500, $1,500, or $5,000 help you instantly remove some pain and financial burdens from your life?

Money doesn't buy you happiness, but it can buy you time, experiences, better access to health, education, higher quality of living, opportunities, generational wealth, and so on.

One of my favorite people to follow on social media is Jimmy Darts. He goes around blessing random people with money for their acts of kindness. Oftentimes, it is only $500, but scrolling through the endless videos, you can see that this money meets an immediate need for people. Many of the people he blesses with money state exactly what they are going to do with that money right away. Some need it to pay rent, buy food, get a bike so they can get a job, etc. I bet if you interviewed them immediately after that experience, they would say the $500 isn't what made them happy, but what that money was going to help them with that leaves them overjoyed. This is what makes watching Jimmy Darts' videos so captivating. You witness the instant relief and the overwhelming joy that money in their hands and the generosity of a stranger produced.

One example is Tommy, a homeless man who was living on the streets of Los Angeles. Jimmy Darts' donation changed the trajectory of his entire life. First, it started with getting him a meal, phone, and hotel. Then, a few adventures, like a day at Disneyland—the very first time Tommy had been there. Then, it led to getting him new teeth and clothing so he could apply for a job. After several weeks of following up and blessing Tommy with over $20,000, he is now off the streets, working as an auto mechanic, which provides a stable income and a sense of purpose. It all started with hopscotch and $500 cash.

Money can have a profound impact on the quality of someone's life. It's a real tool that can provide freedom in many ways.

Perhaps one of the greatest things money can buy is your time. In his book *The Psychology of Money*, author Morgan Housel writes:

> *"The highest form of wealth is the ability to wake up every morning and say, 'I can do whatever I want today.'"*
>
> *"People want to become wealthier to make themselves happier. Happiness is a complicated subject because everyone's different. But if there's a common denominator in happiness—a universal fuel of joy—it's that people want to control their lives."*
>
> *"The ability to do what you want, when you want, with who you want, for as long as you want, is priceless. It is the highest dividend money pays."*

The secret that wealthy people have discovered is that money buys you time, and time is truly freedom. Time to spend with family, time to travel without having to ask for time off, time to take care of your mental and physical health, and time to experience life unburdened by bills, work, and someone else's expectations.

The true flex isn't the zeros in your bank account; it's in the ability to do what you want, when you want, without having to ask for permission. Time is the most precious resource out there. Money comes and goes, but time is finite. Time is the most valuable resource. It's entirely non-renewable. Once today ends, you never get that time back, and we simply don't know when our time here on Earth will be up.

The average person will spend 90,000 hours of their life working. That's roughly 10.2 years. Working and making money is a necessary part of how we live and survive. It's how we provide value, find purpose, and put a roof over our heads.

Our concepts of money and value are deeply intertwined with our concepts of time, and the only way most of us have ever learned to earn income is by trading our time for dollars. The rich have learned the secret to leveraging "Other People's Time" (OPT) and focus on creating businesses and investments that make them money in their sleep. This is how you divorce money and time. This is how you truly find freedom.

It works both ways, too. What if you had all the time in the world but no money? How would you travel? How would you hire help? How could you start a business or invest? Everything in our world requires money.

If you think that more money won't enhance your life, you are living in the "poverty spirit." If you think that someone else's financial situation somehow takes from your abundance, you are in the poverty spirit. The truth is that wealthy people don't worry about these things. They know the value of money and what it can do for them. They have a reverence, appreciation, and respect for this resource and how it can benefit them and the ones they love.

Money matters, and it turns out that it actually can make a lot of people happy.

CHAPTER 3

3 Money Influencers

*"Thoughts become perception, perception becomes reality.
Alter your thoughts, alter your reality."*
–William James, the "Father of American psychology."

Do you ever wonder where your beliefs and behaviors around money started? Have you ever wondered why you might spend more money when you're feeling stressed or anxious? Or maybe you feel yourself being a little stingy with money, holding onto every penny for dear life.

Do you ever get uncomfortable talking about money? Maybe even a little angry or irritable when discussing finances with a friend, family member, or spouse?

Do you ever use phrases like, "That's too expensive," or find yourself justifying your purchase to a friend or family member by reassuring them that you "got such a good deal?"

Our "money life" is complicated. Someone once asked me, "What was the moment or the thing that changed for you that led to your success?" My answer is pretty simple: I had to unlearn everything I ever knew, believed, and heard about money. It wasn't until I could recognize my own behaviors and where they were coming from that I was able to finally feel liberated from the financial hardships and money relationship I had.

It was when I stopped feeling bad for myself and like a victim in life that I was awakened. When I finally took some personal responsibility for my behavior and spending habits. When I could understand and find some perspective as to why I felt certain ways about money or felt jealous of what other people had. I went on an entire journey to understand what shaped my beliefs around money, and it transformed my life. I found healing and clarity.

Budget apps, spreadsheets, or that next MLM opportunity won't get you that financial breakthrough you need until you first address the internal messaging you and others have been telling you. We need to heal from our money wounds just like any other pain, loss, or suffering we have experienced. It isn't until we heal our relationship with money that we can start to unlock the true financial potential in our lives and open the floodgates of Heaven.

In this chapter, I will take you on a journey to understanding what influences your spending, saving, management, and core beliefs around money. I will also provide an opportunity for you to do some exercises to reveal the roadblocks that are in your way. I hope you find relief, forgiveness, and grace as we unlock what's holding you back, and I will give you a simple method for releasing these things once and for all!

The thoughts, feelings, and behaviors you have when it comes to money are shaped by what I call our three money influencers:

- What you *heard* about money.
- What you *learned* about money.
- What you *experienced* around money.

Let's do a deep dive into each of these influencers and reflect on what might be holding you back today.

What You Heard

What you have heard about money has bled into your subconscious for years, often without you even being aware of it. The phrases overheard from family members, friends, and even media and movies all affect your beliefs around money.

Here are some phrases that may sound familiar:

- Money doesn't grow on trees.
- A penny saved is a penny earned.
- Don't want to break the bank.
- Save your money for a rainy day.
- The rich get richer, and the poor get poorer.
- We can't afford it.

I'm sure you can remember the exact place you heard this or the person who has said some of these phrases throughout your lifetime. Maybe you can even hear yourself reiterating these phrases to your family, friends, or your own children.

In my household, my dad had a phrase he always used when I would ask him to buy me something. He would say, "Want in one hand, s#%! in the other. See which one fills up first." First, I apologize; my dad was a little rough around the edges. Second, what the heck does that even mean? As a kid, I interpreted that as meaning the things I want in life still don't amount to crap. He would only say this when I was asking him to buy me something, so how did this shape me?

It made me feel like my desires were worthless. It made me feel guilty for asking because regardless of the context of that phrase, it was always to discourage me from asking for anything again. It shut me down and made me feel like my wants were meaningless.

My parents were very hardworking people. They taught me the value of hard work. They never handed me anything. They made me earn my way at a young age. I was told, "Money doesn't grow on trees," and that if I wanted something, I had to "earn it the hard way."

While hard work builds character, this also only taught me how to become a master at selling my time. It put me into the workforce at eight years of age. That's right - 8. It taught me that if I wanted anything out of life, it was going to be a difficult road ahead. It would be hard: I'd have to earn every penny. And that's exactly what I experienced for nearly two decades. I had two jobs from age 8 to 24. It was common for me to sacrifice sleep and my mental and physical health to earn the money I needed to survive. It was all part of the conditioning I had learned from a young age and the acceptance of the belief that living a comfortable life was always going to involve sacrifice.

This drove me into an endless cycle of having multiple jobs and learning that sacrifice was the cost of success. I was driven to exhaustion and burnout and never felt like I was going to get ahead.

It wasn't until I became aware of how this lesson was driving my life that I was able to pump the brakes and think about the kind of life I wanted to live. I was able to learn to work smarter, not harder, to build the life of my dreams. The hard way isn't always the right way. Once I learned that you could earn money and income while enjoying life and that life didn't have to be so hard, I was able to break free of this generational belief and habit of trading time for dollars.

So, it's time for you to reflect on your own circumstances. I want you to think about what you heard growing up and how you think that is still impacting you today. Don't skip this exercise or dismiss the importance of this chapter. It's only after you have done the inner work that you will be able to experience the outer results.

Exercise:

What were the common money phrases in your household?

_____

_____

_____

_____

_____

How do you think this has impacted your beliefs around money?

_____

_____

_____

_____

_____

What are some of your catchphrases about money?

_____

_____

_____

_____

_____

Do you find these phrases helpful or harmful?

_____

_____

_____

_____

_____

What You Learned

The truth is, we are all so stuck in our own money biases and stories that what we believe about money isn't based on reality at all. Let me share a little story with you.

Every time I would sit down with my husband to track our spending and talk budgets, I would burst into tears.

Overwhelm, guilt, shame, fear, and insecurities all came to the surface *anytime* money would be brought up. But why? Where did this come from?

To answer that, I have to go back to my childhood.

(Mom, if you are reading this, I'm sorry. I love you and know you did all you could to provide for us. I am aware we all have inherited money stories. This is mine.)

My parents were typical middle-class people with good jobs. My dad worked for an electrical company, and my mom worked as a manager at Bank of America. My mom's side of the family had some money. She once told me that she never wore the same outfit twice. She had a full-size balance beam and parallel bars in her backyard because she was a pretty good gymnast, and I would think you needed some serious money to be able to have that kind of personal training equipment.

My mom got married at 18. She left behind her parents' hopes of her being an Olympic gymnast and moved to the middle of California's Mojave desert with my dad. She was even offered a horse, which she had wanted her whole life, on the condition that she leave my dad. I guess being a rebel against your parents really runs in our blood.

My grandmother died when my mom was pregnant with me. It would be many years later that her father would pass away, leaving behind a pretty big inheritance for my mom and her two siblings. Without stirring up too much family drama, my mom would never see any significant amount of that family inheritance.

My dad's side was the typical working family. My grandpa worked for Shell Oil as a chemist and provided a comfortable suburban life for his family, and my grandmother had her Amway side hustle. Even up until my grandmother's passing, she would have shelves of Amway products in her office and place reorders with her Rolodex of customers over her rotary phone. I can see where I got my work ethic from.

That's a little background, so no one thinks I came from a trust fund of family wealth. I mean, it would have been nice, and there's nothing wrong with that, but Ryan and I have worked *hard* for everything we have obtained, and we weren't raised with silver spoons in our mouths.

But something significant happened in my life around high school. My mom took me back-to-school shopping, but this wasn't like any other time we'd done it before. You see, I was somewhat of a tomboy growing up. Until the first few years in high school, I wore Vans, baggy jeans, and men's tee shirts. I was not a girly girl, but heading into my junior year, I finally embraced my feminine side. So when I told my mom I wanted to get some dresses for school, she went all out. *Finally*, she would get the girly girl she could shop with and spoil, so it was a blast!

We went from store to store in the mall and picked outfits off of the mannequins, and I felt like royalty. Besides a few disagreements on styles and tastes—like every mother and daughter have—she let me get everything I asked for. I walked out of the mall feeling like Julia Roberts in *Pretty Woman*—arms full!

It was such a fun experience, and one I still remember to this day. So when we got home, I couldn't wait to hang up all my new clothes and pick out my outfit for my first day. But when we pulled up to the house, and before I could open the car door, my mom said something to me that would change everything: "We are going to wait until your dad is asleep to bring in all these bags. When he's asleep, I want you to bring it all in, hang it up, and don't tell your daddy."

Immediately, I felt this sense that I had done something wrong. Was he not going to like what I picked out? Was it that we didn't have the money for all this stuff? Was my mom lying to my dad about money? What had I just done? Were we OK? I thought to myself, *I don't need any of this stuff; let's just take it back.*

I never talked about that moment with my mom until a few years ago, when I was searching for understanding about the guilt I had when it came to buying clothes. What I discovered was pretty interesting. It turns out that my dad knew about every penny they spent, and he totally didn't care. My parents didn't hide money from each other, and my mom had nothing to feel bad about. But during this conversation with my mom, she remembered something interesting: she recalls her mom telling her to do the same exact thing when she was a kid. She had an abusive father and wasn't allowed to wear makeup. She would wash her face off after school before heading home to avoid being punished or beaten. She had learned to hide and lie to her father at a young age, which is what she was inadvertently teaching me.

So not only was this a generational lesson passed on from my grandmother to my mother and then to me, but it continued to be reinforced a few other times in my life. Fast forward to my young adult life, and I would see that same story play over and over in my decade of working in retail.

Working in retail, I imagine, is very similar to being a hairstylist. You get *all* the juicy details about someone's life, and usually, they are shopping to blow off steam or for a little retail therapy. I worked in some of the most affluent retail locations in the country—Soho, New York, Robertson

Boulevard, Larchmont, The Americana at Brand, and The Grove. I worked with celebrity clients like Paris Hilton, Katy Perry, and Faith Hill. The people I was attending to had a lot of money.

But so many times, I would be asked to cut the tags off of items so their husbands didn't know, or use a different credit card their husband wouldn't see, or skip the bag or tissue paper and just shove it in this reusable bag so their husband wouldn't see them bring it in.

There it was again, the same story. Other people were also adhering to the story I had learned back in high school. But why?

Was it true that their husbands would get angry or upset with them? It was usually the total opposite when women would shop *with* their husbands. The husband would encourage them and compliment them when they came out of the fitting room. I never saw these versions of angry men telling their women what they can and can't buy.

Then why was there so much guilt and shame? Why was I cutting tags, and what were these women so stressed out about?

Fast forward a few more years, and I started to want to learn more about women, business, and money. I started reading articles about the wealthiest women in history. I learned how many of them built their wealth, the businesses they started, and the glass ceilings they shattered. I devoured any book I could get my hands on that taught me wealth principles, entrepreneurship, money mindset, and investing strategies and told me stories of the wealthiest people in the world. I was hooked and also kind of confused.

There was such a different message in these books than what I had learned growing up. Certainly, none of these concepts and ideas were discussed at school, my church or in Bible studies. As I started off on this journey, I would ask church leader after church leader how I could learn more about what God says about money and entrepreneurship. The pastor's wife was a female business owner with a multi-million-dollar company. I asked her to start a Bible study on women in the marketplace. She was flattered but told me she had never even thought of doing that before. She had been in business and ministry for over 20 years! Time and time again, I would just be pointed to the same limited resources.

But inside these books, studies, and programs, I couldn't escape the feelings of guilt and shame. In fact, now I felt those things even more. I would get through a study and feel like a moron who just needed to cut up all my credit cards and stop buying coffee. There it is again - the coffee. It's always the coffee. I guess I just can't handle money, and I never will. Interestingly enough, the business resources I had consumed never mentioned any of these strategies as a way to financial freedom. Often, they spoke more about taking a leap of faith, pushing through fear, and taking risks to reach their goals—exactly the opposite of what I was learning at home or at church.

I was once handed a book by a pastor. To be fair, he was never taught anything about money, business, or investing as it relates to the Bible and church, but I'll never forget it.

Inside this book, I read a story about a real-life example of a woman who had worked her way up to a high position at the company and was now being considered for a promotion. The whole point of this chapter was to discuss the "proper" way to handle this situation from the perspective of the owner who wanted to promote her and how he was to navigate this as a man of God.

The preface was that the owner was seeking advice from a Christian leader on whether or not he should promote this woman because the job would require her to travel more. The "challenge" was that this would have two implications. The first is that she would be away from home more, and this was concerning because she had children. The second was that she would be traveling with other male team members, which would mean there would be hotels and arrangements that might compromise the team's moral values. The Christian leader advised him not to promote her after all. I was so disappointed because after years of searching within the church—and I mean many different churches and leaders—here's what I really started learning about the perceptions of women, money, and success.

I learned our husband has the final say on what we can do with our money. He is the leader of the household, after all, so just submit and leave it all to him.

Women just shop too much. We buy too many coffees and are completely financially irresponsible. If we want to try investing, just hire a guy at Edward Jones. This is safe and reliable, and we should leave it up to the man in the suit who knows far more than us.

Also, remember it's easier for a camel to get through the eye of a needle than for someone who is rich to enter the Kingdom of God, so make sure you don't become rich.

Women aren't capable of managing both a home and a career. That's just too much.

Also, women should never travel with men who aren't their husbands. Ever. Or they should sacrifice what they have worked for and make sure they don't tempt the men in their office. Remember, this only pertains to women. Men have no problem balancing their careers and leading the home. And, after all, men are basically just dumb, predictable robots. They are completely incapable of respect and self-control when women are near. They are like the love-stricken skunk Pepé Le Pew from *Looney Tunes* around *all* women, so it's obviously the woman's responsibility not to cause them temptation.

I wish I was making this up. The more resources I was being pointed to, the more disappointed and discouraged I became. Don't worry; I never gave the book back to the pastor—I threw it in the trash and asked God for forgiveness.

But this is what we are up against. These are the types of beliefs we learn along the way, and I'm only just scratching the surface of the issues, lessons, biases, and misinformation that are being projected.

The truth is there is something that is holding us back, and it's something I found myself thinking about for way too long.

Is it worth it to be a better manager of my finances?

Is it worth it to invest?

Is it worth it to ask for a raise?

Is it worth it to charge what I'm worth?

Is it worth it to make money?

The answer to all these questions is a simple *"Yes."*

The question isn't, *"Is it worth it?"*

The question you should be asking yourself is, *"Am I worth it?"*

We all come from our own background of money stories and experiences, and we would be naive to think these stories don't shape our behavior and beliefs around who we are, what's important, and what we are worth.

As women, we are so busy trying not to ruffle any feathers and feel bad that we don't feel deserving or worthy of the desires God has placed in our hearts, and that especially includes money. We've learned to think of the common good, put others first, and that making ourselves a priority is selfish.

There is so much to unlearn and so much doubt to surrender. But there is peace in knowing the truth. You are worthy. You are enough. You are capable. You are deserving. You are blessed. You can make a difference.

Are you ready to transform your life and rewrite your story for good? I want to share a super simple exercise with you that has helped hundreds of my clients rewrite their story and find freedom around the beliefs that they have about money. It's called my "MIX Shift Framework." Here's how it works.

The "M" Stands for Message

What is the message you have believed about money based on your experience? What do you keep telling yourself?

Examples:

"I'm not that good with money."

"Wanting money means I'm not content."

"I feel like God is punishing me. Other people are seeing His blessings, but I must be doing something wrong."

The "I" Stands for "Is This Message True?"

Yes or no?

Most likely the answer is no. Maybe there are parts of the message that feel true, and you can acknowledge that, but we are trying to dive deeper into where these beliefs come from and how they have shaped us.

The "X" Stands for Cross It Out

That old message you keep telling yourself? Draw a line right through it. Here's where you write your new story or belief about that message.

Examples:

~~"I'm not that good with money."~~

"I'm growing in my confidence with money every day."

~~"Wanting money means I'm not content."~~

"I can desire more abundance *and* be grateful for all that I currently have."

~~"I feel like God is punishing me. Other people are seeing His blessings, but I must be doing something wrong."~~

"God is for me, not against me. My stewardship and faith are growing. God will bless me beyond what I ever imagined. God knows the desires of my heart, and I trust Him fully."

Exercise:

Now that you know how this experience has shaped your relationship with money, use the "MIX Shift Framework" to rewrite your *new* story.

M: What is the *message* you have believed about money based on this experience?

_____

_____

_____

_____

I: *Is* this message true? (Yes or No)

_____

_____

_____

_____

X: Now *X* (cross out) that old message and answer what is actually true about this message/belief? What would I rather be telling myself?

_____

_____

_____

_____

What You Experienced

Can you remember a time in your life that changed everything you felt about money? Was there something that happened: a foreclosure, a business failure, a divorce, a bankruptcy, a childhood memory that you remember so vividly that you can picture yourself there right now? Remember specific details about that moment, like what you were wearing or who was surrounding you. Just thinking about this moment, you have a rush of emotions, as if you were reliving that moment all over again.

I call this a money event. It's an experience you had that burned you. It hurt, brought you pain, and forever changed the way you felt about money. It brings on emotions like fear, shame, guilt, and embarrassment. If you've been in this place, you know exactly what I am talking about—you're thinking of that very moment right now. All the memories of that event come rushing back to you, and it's like you are there all over again.

I had this event in 2014 when I walked away from a business venture that would cost me $400,000, a lawsuit of ten years, and the kind of wounds that take a decade to heal. I can remember the horror of that final day I stepped foot at that business. The crisp fall morning, the sun shining, and a slight breeze in the air. The quietness of the barn into which I had put my blood, sweat, and tears. I planed every board of wood on that building and can literally smell the stain as I sit here remembering it. Even the minute details from the pile of mail sitting on my lap that I could barely make clear through the sea of tears dripping down my face as we turned left off of the property, never to return.

In fact, this event would cost me years of living out my full potential. I certainly didn't think I was capable of teaching anyone about business when I had just lost one. How could I share about money when this event nearly made us bankrupt? I could write a whole other book about all the self-doubt, heartache, and mental battles I've had and things that still come up that made this event pivotal in how I viewed money and assessed future risks.

This event impacted not only my beliefs but also those of the people involved in this business. My husband became distrustful of partners and doing deals with other people. He started to look at all the worst-case scenarios in all our real estate investing because we had thought we had worked every angle, crossed every T, and had a fail-proof plan to prevent anything like this from happening. We both let this event keep us from venturing out of our comfort zones for years. We went back to what we were comfortable with and took some valuable lessons with us along the way.

Money events aren't always huge ones, either. They are sometimes quiet and seemingly innocent events. I know this example is going to seem silly, but the other day, I bought some nail polish. I hadn't purchased nail polish in years. I've either had acrylic nails or gotten a pedicure a few times a year. I found the section in Target and started looking for the right color. Then I saw the brand Essie and immediately had a flashback: I was working in retail and was on my break. I stopped at a beauty supply store on my way back to work. And there it was, this beautiful bottle of confetti nail polish. It was called "Cake Batter," and it was all the rage. The only problem was that it was like an $18 dollar bottle of nail polish, and I was broke. I was making $55,000 at my manager job, but my rent and student loans were about $2,000 a month alone, so you could imagine I didn't have a miscellaneous envelope filled with cash to pull from and purchase this overpriced bottle of glitter.

So what did I do? I cried. It wasn't really about the nail polish. It was yet another reminder of how broke I was, how desperate I felt, and how embarrassed I was that I couldn't even pay $18 for a stupid bottle of nail polish. I can think of several mini-events just like this one that impacted me and my confidence around money.

Now, I'm nearing 40 years old, standing in the nail polish aisle at Target, looking at the same brand of polish. I take a moment to relive my money story and reflect on how far I've come. I smile to myself because it felt like the end of the world back when I was living in it, and it sure is interesting how temporary our circumstances really are. I grab a bottle of nude nail polish (because now I'm boring) and walk to the register.

What I learned is that these money events can completely change your life, for better or for worse, but they don't have to define your future.

Once I became aware of my money events and was able to see how it all has impacted me, I could only start to heal, learn, grow, and let them refine me.

I want you to think about the money events or experiences you've had, big or small, that are shaping you today and how you feel and act around money. The first step to growing your financial confidence is awareness. The next step is rewriting them so they don't have a stranglehold on your abundant future.

It's time to rewrite your story. I want you to take some time to write out your money event. It's literally what I did when writing this chapter. Get angry, let out a good cry, laugh, and share your revelation with someone you trust! The abundance you are searching for is on the other side of that story.

CHAPTER 4

Not Your Fault

"The secret of getting ahead is getting started."
–Mark Twain

For much of my life, I've been curious about what makes people rich. What's the secret sauce that gives some the ability to have "stupid money"? The kind of money that allows you to buy islands, a luxury yacht, fly on your private jet, and befriend some of the richest in the world. The kind of money that makes $20,000 feel like 20 bucks.

In my curiosity, I couldn't help but feel like there was a hidden secret to amassing that much wealth. These kinds of people have to have some esoteric knowledge, which is inaccessible to others like me. There must be something I was missing or lacking because other people have been able to figure it out. I must not be educated enough. They must be geniuses with ridiculously high IQs. They probably came from family money. They must have been invited into private rooms and conversations where this secret is revealed, and only a few of the lucky ones will get to experience it.

I felt decades behind, and like I would never figure this money game out. I've spent years devouring books on wealth and success, studying stories of how people started their businesses, and listening to some of the most influential, successful, and wealthy people in our history. Here's what I realized: *no one is born with financial literacy*. We aren't taught these skills in school. We don't learn about money and success in church. Most of us don't have examples of what total financial freedom looks like in our own families, and when we do, often that knowledge isn't passed down.

Some people have major advantages, and others overcome seemingly impossible circumstances. Our journeys might be different, but there's one thing we all have in common: we aren't born smart with money. No one comes out of the womb a financial expert. Every single wealthy and successful person has had to learn and earn these skills. They can only be acquired through experience, trials, and tribulations: by having money, losing money, learning, unlearning, breaking money stories, and having the courage to go for it despite a world that sees this venture as selfish and self-serving.

We are all on this journey of life trying to discover our purpose and find fulfillment. It might feel at times like you are just trying not to drown in a sea of crashing waves. It might feel impossible to keep treading water, and it might feel like you are all alone in this big ocean. You aren't the only one trying to figure this money thing out, and it's not exactly your fault for not being as far ahead as you would like to, either. With so little financial literacy out there, you might feel a little behind. You might feel like it's too late for you or like you are at a disadvantage, but that couldn't be further from the truth.

Not only are we taught very little information when it comes to money, wealth building, and retirement, but as Morgan Housel puts it in his book *The Psychology of Money*, "The entire concept of being entitled to retirement is, at most, two generations old."

Housel does an amazing job breaking down the history of our current financial system and how we arrived where we are today. For example, he points out, "The 401(k)—the backbone savings vehicle of American retirement—did not exist until 1978. The Roth IRA was not born until 1998. It should surprise no one that many of us are bad at saving and investing for retirement. We're not crazy. We're all just newbies."

Isn't that a relief?! I'm not trying to dismiss the importance of taking personal responsibility for your circumstances and taking action to change them, but I do hope this offers you some insight as to why you feel behind or "out of the loop."

Now, let's think about that in terms of women and the history of our financial institutions. Many of these savings and retirement strategies were created by men, for men, and women were simply left out of the conversation. It might not have been malicious. That's just how it happened. Not only is the financial infrastructure we know fairly new, but it wasn't created with women in mind.

Before 1974, women were not legally permitted to obtain a mortgage without a male co-signer. It wasn't until President Reagan signed the Women's Business Ownership Act in 1988 that women were able to get a business loan without a male co-signer. The Equal Pay Act was passed in 1963, requiring men and women to be paid equally when doing the same work. It wasn't until the Equal Credit Opportunity Act was passed in 1974—that's over ten years later—that women were able to get credit cards in their own name.

I want you to think about that for a second. What year was your mother born? Likely, your mother was the first woman in your family who was able to get access to credit of her own, purchase a house, or get a business loan by herself. That means we're only the second generation of women to have access to money! It's not that we aren't good with money, it's that we've only just started.

It's been less than 50 years! So, while you might be feeling all of this frustration and anger about pay gaps and missed opportunities, and you aren't seeing a lot of women in the rooms that you want to be in, it's because we're just getting in the game. Give yourself a little bit of grace and understand that the financial framework as a whole is fairly new and even newer to us women.

Not only have we started the race late, but society has played a large role in perpetuating a lot of noise when it comes to women and money. We are told that husbands are breadwinners and a woman's place is only in the home. And because the natural tendency of most men is to protect and provide for their families, we've been told at a young age that a man will be there to take care and provide for us. We've been positioned as weak and in need of a man to rescue us.

It's scripted into endless Disney movie plots: The princess needs saving and awaits her Prince Charming to come rescue her.

Boys are encouraged at a young age to take risks, think out of the box, and push the norm. It's seen as creative and adventurous. Their childhood toys focus on engineering, building, and creating.

Young girls are taught to be safe and polite. It's not nice to speak up. Don't outshine others. Our toys don't necessarily spark innovation or encourage us to strengthen our minds.

What about women who have accomplished incredible success? How many of them have achieved greatness just to be met with, "What does your husband do?" Our personal success has often been attributed to a male's financial backing.

I've read endless stories of multimillionaire female investors and founders who've had to contend with assumptions that they had Daddy's money, or they got some alimony to get started. They obviously couldn't achieve anything on their own merits.

On one occasion, I was at the bank with my husband. We were getting ready to sign closing documents on another investment. At this point, we owned at least 50 properties, and it wasn't my first rodeo. I looked at the male banker across from me and asked him a very specific question about the market and interest rate trends.

He acknowledged my question, then proceeded to look at my husband to answer it. It took me a second to realize what was happening, and at first, I wanted to give him the benefit of the doubt that he was simply addressing both of us. But after several minutes of replying to my husband with the answer, I leaned over slightly, right at eye level, to grab his attention as if to say, "Hi. I asked the question. Why are you answering to him?"

I don't blame the banker. I don't think he was trying to insult me. He was simply so used to talking to the husband about financial matters that this was just another one of those customers. There are also a lot of women who don't make the financial decisions in their relationships. They leave the financial responsibility to the man and have no clue where their money is. I've had countless conversations with women who choose to stay passive with their money and rely on their husbands to make the best decisions for them, so maybe the banker assumed I was one of those women.

If I'm being honest, for many years, I was. I thought my husband must be smarter and more capable than me. I don't know why. He didn't take any financial courses in college. He started investing in real estate without knowing how. We were literally learning together, reading the same books, and doing deals together. We followed the same learning curve and built a multimillion-dollar portfolio together, and I still felt inadequate. It took me years to take back my financial power and realize I too, was smart and capable. It took me years to build up enough courage to even call myself an investor. I recently started playing pickleball, and my favorite time to play is in the early afternoon. I'm usually the youngest one there around that time, and at least a few times a week, someone gets curious enough to ask me what I do for a living that I can be playing pickleball two to three times a week at 1:00 p.m. on a weekday. When I tell them I am a real estate investor, they always assume that means I am a real estate agent, and then the follow-up goes a little something like, "How about those interest rates, huh?" So I started telling people I was retired, but that just got some polite laughs. If they pry a little further, I tell them I have rentals, flip houses, and own some apartment buildings. That usually leads to, "What does your husband do?" You get where this is going.

I've had to advocate for myself endless times at the bank, with title companies, in loan meetings, and with contractors. Unfortunately, I know my story isn't unique. These societal norms are so ingrained in us that we actually believe them.

Even as I write this, there's a viral movement going around called "Girl Math." It makes me want to cringe because it's perpetuating this narrative that girls are dumb with money.

These videos go something like this:

"Girl Math"

If something costs less than I thought it would, I can go buy something else to make the difference, and it's fine.

If I return something that I bought, then I will make money.

Anything under $5 is basically free.

I bought something for $38, which means it was only $30.

If my favorite clothing store is having a sale, I have to buy something, or I am actually losing money.

If my Starbucks app is loaded, the coffee is free.

If I buy a $300 purse but use it every single day, it will cost me less than a dollar a day, which is basically free.

If you buy something with cash, it's free.

Going to an event or concert is free because I purchased the tickets so long ago that it doesn't even count.

If I pay someone back for dinner and there's money in my Venmo, dinner is free.

I get that this was supposed to be funny, and I'm not entirely humorless, but if I'm being honest, this trend generalizes women as irresponsible shopaholics. Much of comedy is based on truth, which is what makes it relatable and funny. I don't think it's funny to make unintelligent decisions that harm our financial well-being and then make viral TikToks that help us justify these behaviors. It's embarrassing. It should be called "Justified Math" instead, and here's the kicker: men do it too. People will look for any excuse to justify overspending or buying things they don't need. I find it infuriating and insulting that we're dumbing down women's ability to be excellent money managers. And we believe it, too!

This idea that we "aren't good with money" has seeped into our subconscious on so many levels. Here are some interesting statistics that show just how much our lack of confidence in ourselves is keeping us from the abundance equally available to us.

> "Financial insecurity may be a key reason that only 26% of American women invest in the stock market, despite 41% of these same women viewing the market positively."
>
> –S&P Global

> "As of 2021, only 33% of women actually see themselves as investors. And only 42% feel confident in their ability to save for future milestones like retirement."
>
> –Fidelity

> "Only 9% of women think they make better investors than men, despite research showing that they earn consistently better returns."
>
> –The Motley Fool

So why do we dumb it down by doing viral TikTok videos when, statistically, we are better investors than men, and we have every ability to excel in our financial lives, too?

Despite these statistics, we still feel like someone else will be better with our money. We continue to give up our financial power. We think, *Oh well, that financial advisor at Merrill Lynch, they probably know more than I do. They've got a business, they wear a tie, and they have the certification on their wall that proves they know what they are doing. They must be super smart at investing.*

I've got some interesting statistics about that, too. Eighty to 90% of financial advisors go out of business within three years. This means only 10%–20% of financial advisors are ultimately successful.

Here's another fun fact: many stockbrokers are salesmen, not investors. Depending on how their contracts are structured, many are rewarded when they meet their sales target, meaning they make their money on commission. Their bonuses are based on the clients they sign. Their business card might have the title of "financial adviser," but like a car salesman at a dealership, they are salespeople. Only fiduciary financial advisors are required to place your best interests above their own. They must follow certain rules and regulations.

A fiduciary is someone who manages money or property for someone else. When you're named a fiduciary and accept the role, you must—by law—manage the person's money and property for their benefit, not yours.[3]

Want to guess how many of the 385,058 registered investment advisors in the U.S. are true fiduciary investment advisors?

A whopping 11.2%![4]

But here, we still trust financial institutions, financial advisors, and more men who are in suits with our money. One of the biggest false beliefs is that the stock market is the safest place to invest. This is one of the only investment strategies that you hear people talk about because people are making money from the stock market whether you make money or not. Your financial planner still makes money on your money even when you lose money. A study done over 15 years found that 95% of the time, fund managers do a worse job than if you invested in index funds yourself.[5]

That means only 5% of all financial planners beat the market. Forty-six percent of financial planners have no retirement plan of their own. There's nothing wrong with investing in the stock market, and it can be a good place to build wealth and prepare for your financial future. But when we continue to give up our financial power, assuming other people have more interest in our success financially than we do, we're not learning anything. We aren't even getting in the game.

If you're solely relying on your financial advisor, your partner, a parent, or just waiting for someone else to come save you because you think someone else cares more than you, knows more than you, and has the secret formula to financial freedom, it's time to wake up. You are robbing yourself of the financial confidence, skills, and literacy you need to transform your "money life." Here's the cold, hard truth they failed to teach us in the movies: no one is coming to save you.

No one will care more about your money than you—and no one *should* care more about your money than you.

Society has a lot of narratives around women and money that we need to overcome, but we have a lot of work to do when it comes to the inner game of wealth.

We need to stop believing things like, *I'm not good with money*. We need to remove thoughts like, *I don't like numbers*. We need to recognize that when we say, "I think there is money in my account," we have stopped taking radical responsibility for our lives and will continue to fall victim to our circumstances.

Those thoughts and beliefs that perpetuate our behaviors around our financial lives are what fuel our insecurity.

If you get anything from this chapter, I want you to give yourself some grace.

As women, we've had a lot working against us. When it comes to finances, investing, business, money markets, and retirement plans, we haven't been included for most of our history. We've had to combat inequality. We've had to combat societal norms, narratives, and movies that continue to shape our confidence and beliefs around money. It's time that we rewrite our stories. It's time that we forgive ourselves. It's time to stop blaming others or our circumstances. It's time that we release the pressure of feeling like we are failing, that we aren't _____ enough—fill in the blank with whatever terms are appropriate to you. It's time to stop talking ourselves down.

The real secret some of the most successful people in the world have figured out is that they stopped playing around and started playing to compete. They got serious about what they wanted from life and made a decision to play to win. I think it's about time we get in the game, too, don't you?

CHAPTER 5

No One Will Save You

"The most common way people give up their power is by thinking they don't have any." –Alice Walker, author of The Color Purple

Let me share how I almost died at the age of seven and lost $30,000 at age 18. When I was seven years old, I was in a horrific car accident with my mom. We were hit head-on by a drunk driver after we had just dropped my sister off at school. In a split second, my mom pulled over as far as she could, reached her arm across my body to shield me, and *boom!* I can remember the pitch darkness I was sent into, as the impact was so hard I had blacked out. It was quiet. I remember feeling peaceful, and I remember vividly seeing this tiny tunnel of light. It's one of the most weightless and free moments of my life. For what I am sure, it was only a few seconds, but it felt like hours; I was in a totally different place.

What came next felt like someone hit the rewind button, and I could faintly hear, "Neener! Neener! Neener!" No, it wasn't some school kids teasing me. Neener was a nickname only my mom and dad called me. My mom was shaking my limp body and yelling at me in sheer panic. I woke up in pure terror, like when you do sometimes when you are having a nightmare, but unfortunately, this time, I wasn't dreaming. I opened my eyes to my mom's face, which was cut up from hitting the windshield, and all I could see was the whites in her eyes through all the blood. I screamed and started crying. Some people had seen the accident happen, and they pulled me from the car and laid me down on the side of the road. I remember my stomach hurting, and I could just hear my mom yelling in pain. We were several miles from town, and the nearest hospital was hours away. The car had hit us head-on and went over our car, with my mom taking the majority of the impact. They had to use the jaws of life to get her out. My mom had broken ribs, two lacerations across her face, a torn rotator cuff from reaching over to protect me, a collapsed lung, and she had to stay in the ICU for a week. I got to walk out of that hospital that night with my dad with nothing worse than a sore body—praise the Lord.

The Lord saved my life that day. You see, the car my mom was driving never had a proper working passenger seat belt. I wasn't allowed to sit up front with my mom because of it. She had just had the seat belt fixed on Wednesday, and our accident occurred that Saturday. Three days before, I would have been sitting in the back, right behind my mom, like I always did. That day, we dropped off my sister, and I asked to sit up front with my mom. Since the belt was fixed, she let me move. When we got to see the car after the accident, the entire roof of the car collapsed behind my mom. Had my sister been in the car, or had the seatbelt not been fixed, I would have been crushed and killed on impact.

I can remember the first time I got to meet the man who had hit us. All three of us survived the crash, and we lived in a small town. I don't know why my dad felt like he needed to meet the man who almost took two of the three women in his life from him, but he did. I remember the pure sorrow and regret this elderly man had when he looked at me with tears in his eyes and said, "I'm so sorry." I never saw him again.

Through a lawsuit, I was entitled to $30,000, which was to remain in a bank account I could not touch until I was 18. So now you know how I got the money, let me share how I lost it.

When I was applying to colleges, my parents asked me what I wanted to do with my life. I had wanted to be an actress for a very long time. I hadn't been in any plays. I had been an athlete most of my life at this point, and I could probably get a scholarship for track and field, but I wanted to move to Hollywood and be in movies. My parents kindly suggested I go to community college and figure out what I wanted to do. I told them I wanted to be an actress. So then they suggested I think about a "real job" and apply to schools for that. I hadn't thought of anything else, so the only thing that came to mind was: I love the ocean, so if I have to be in school for the next four years, I'll apply to schools for marine biology along the coast of California.

Meanwhile, it was my junior year, and I knew if I wanted to be an actress, I needed to start practicing. So, I quit track my senior year, which was a big shock to my coach, family, and teammates. At the time I quit, I held four school records, had attended state championships in all four of my main events as a freshman, and was well on my way to earning a scholarship. But track wasn't what I wanted to do with my life. I wanted to be an actress.

I auditioned for my first play and got a part in a musical. I started to do some extra work on TV shows and movie sets and even earned my SAG card before I graduated. I *loved* it. Everyone else thought I was crazy for giving up track and field. My coach was so mad at that time he made it a goal to wipe my school records off the wall. (He didn't, by the way—I still hold a few of them to this day.) So when I got an acceptance letter from LMU in Marina del Rey, it was time to really sit down with my parents and talk about school.

I didn't want to go to college. I wanted to move out to the city, go on auditions, get discovered by a talent agent, and be the next Julia Roberts. That was it. So when I told my parents for the billionth time that is what I wanted to do, they caved in and said fine—*but* you still need to go to a college and get a degree for acting. Wait what? I didn't have enough experience to apply for a performing arts school. That wasn't part of my plan. How was I going to pay for that? Aren't those schools expensive?

The next piece of advice I got would change my life forever. I was told I needed to go to college, get a degree, and go to the best school possible for that degree if I wanted to be successful. Well, I did want to be successful, so I followed their advice. I applied for a private university in Orange County, auditioned, and got accepted. I was so excited. It was only after we went to enroll that I realized my parents hadn't been saving up for me to go to college, and now I was in the financial aid building signing a piece of paper that I agreed to the $50,000 a year tuition to attend this school.

There was absolutely no conversation about the money or what type of support I was getting. I had no scholarships or student aid. I could do this "work-study" thing, where I'd work on campus, that would save me a few thousand dollars—and oh, I had $30,000 in a bank account that I just now got access to. Do you know I never even saw that money in the bank, knew the account number, or had a debit card to use any of it? The first time I ever wrote a check in my life was to Chapman University in the amount of $30,000.

That was the first time I gave up my financial power, but it wouldn't be the last.

It's absurd to say out loud, "I spent $200,000 for college to get a theater degree." A theater degree! I'm not a doctor, I'm not even a very good actress, and in two out of four of those years, I was learning basic stage direction and technical lighting. This is how I know that getting into this college was a scam. I applied to a "prestigious" university via an essay and a single audition. I didn't even know how to write a proper essay at the time, so I don't think that's what convinced the admissions office to let me in. But here's how my audition went. I decided to audition with William Shakespeare's famous Hamlet monologue "To be or not to be." I was so nervous for the audition and rightfully so.

Up to this point, I had been in one, just one, musical as a senior in high school. That was my total experience acting in an actual role—ever. Other than that, I had done some extra work on a few television shows with Disney. So here I was on the biggest stage I had ever seen or stepped foot on, with an entire auditorium of seats and three professors I could hardly make out through the bright spotlight shining on me. They asked a few questions to break the ice and told me to start whenever I felt ready. My heart was pounding out of my chest, and my body was shaking. I have only ever rehearsed these lines in front of my main audience, which included my mom, dad, and two miniature dachshunds. Here it goes…

"To be, or not to be, that is the question:
Whether 'tis nobler in the mind to suffer
The slings and arrows of outrageous fortune,
Or to take arms against a sea of troubles
And by opposing end them…"
(Awkward pause)
"And by opposing end them…"
(Another awkward pause…)
"To die…"
(longest pause of my life…)

I'm thinking to myself, *Shoot, I forgot the line. What's next? They're just staring at me. How long have I stood here not said anything? Come on Janine, remember…* Then, after what feels like 10 minutes of absolute dead silence in the auditorium, I hear… "It's ok; take a deep breath and try again."

I took a deep breath and started from the beginning. Now, I can't remember a thing about the next five-minute audition. I blacked out, rushed through my lines, and got it over with as quickly as I could. I wanted to get off that stage so fast and just wait for the rejection letter to arrive in a few weeks. I don't think there was even a sympathy applause. They thanked me for coming, and I left in tears. I wish I could say that I turned it around, blew them out of the water, and ended with a standing ovation because they knew they had just discovered the next Meryl Streep, but I can assure you of one thing— I tanked that audition and there's absolutely no way I would have accepted myself into this school off that performance.

A few weeks later, I received a letter in the mail from Chapman University, *"Congratulations, you have been accepted into the performing arts school."* No way! I was shocked, but knowing what I know now, I am sure I was just another acceptance to meet their tuition quota. There is absolutely no way I should have been accepted into that program.

What's even worse is I think I am the only performing arts major who graduated with a performing arts degree and was never once in a single show at the university. A requirement for graduation was that I be in a mainstage performance, but my college had to make an exception for me. I had to work to put myself through college and wasn't able to make evening rehearsals or take time off for the actual live performances. I was so busy working to pay for the degree I was getting that I couldn't even do the one thing I was there to do—act. How insane is that?

When I graduated from college, I couldn't wait to finally start auditioning and be in a show. I finally felt free. I felt like I had checked the box everyone told me I needed, the one everyone convinced me I would fail without. Little did I know my joy would be met with an entirely different reality.

I was so excited to move to Los Angeles and start acting. I felt like I had waited four years, and now I had a resume with *"Chapman University Graduate"* on it, so casting directors would surely see the value in that. Bet you can guess where I am going. No one cared what school I went to. They wanted to know about my experience (of which I had very little), and I needed to look the part. It took just a few months of going on auditions before I realized I needed to get a consistent job fast.

Once I graduated, my student loan payments kicked in, and I had to start paying $1,200 a month. At the time, that was more than my rent. So, while those first few months felt like bliss as I went on auditions, I wasn't going to be able to pay my bills without a consistent paycheck and job—or, in my case, I would need two if I was going to be able to pay my student loan payment, rent, and all the other expenses that came with living in L.A.

So, by day, I worked as a retail store manager, and by night, I waitressed. I thought it would be temporary until I landed a role. The weeks turned into months, and months turned into years. There I was again, working 15 hours a day, seven days a week. The jobs had replaced the auditions. I felt trapped in this never-ending cycle of paying the price for college, still unable to do the very thing I wanted to. I was chasing dollars instead of my dreams.

I used to believe that I wasn't good with money. I thought I must have missed something that other people learned in their lives, at school, or from their parents. I believed that wealthy people *must* know some elusive secrets to building wealth and generating mass amounts of money that I would just never figure out. Paired with the guilt I had of being in so much debt coming out of college, this just made me feel incompetent. At the time, my sister was the only one close to me who seemed to have it all together. She was married with kids, had bought a house, and always had a budget for visiting me, taking her family to Disneyland, birthdays, and Christmas. So I did what many baby sisters do: I called my sister for help.

I was so desperate and had called her enough times crying over my financial hardships that my sweet sister was willing to do anything to help me figure out how to be better with money. She had gone through a class with her church that used this "Envelope System" for budgeting your money, saving, and something called "snowballing" your debt.

This was the approach she had been using to be more prepared for unexpected expenses and budgeting for her family of five. Little did I know, she was barely surviving too. Over a series of late-night calls we had set up a whole spreadsheet. One side had all my bills, arranged according to when in the month they were due, and another section had my income and when I would get paid every two weeks. Seems simple enough.

It was not until the spreadsheet revealed how broke I was, how bad I was with money, and how, no matter how hard I worked, I would never have enough. It just confirmed what I already knew: I was broke.

I didn't understand. I was the only one I knew who paid their own way through college (private university, for that matter), the only one working two to three jobs while going to college, and the only one of my peers who was paying $1,200 a month in student loans right out of college. In my early days of living in Los Angeles, all I ever did was work. Having two to three jobs was normal for me, but no matter how hard I worked, I just couldn't get ahead.

It didn't matter how hard I tried. No matter how many times I told my friends I couldn't go to the movies with them or passed on dinner nights, I knew I was going to hear from my sister at the end of the week that I was still broke. I lost count of the number of times I would be in the line at Starbucks with knots in my stomach, thinking about all the empty "envelopes" at home. I felt helpless.

On this occasion, I gave up my financial power by trying to get someone else to help me budget my money and figure it out. The only problem was she was just as broke as me. At the time, I didn't know she had just come off living on food stamps or that I was actually making more money at my retail management job than she was with her teaching degree. She was in debt for a very expensive 500-person wedding that she thought our parents were paying, only to be surprised to receive a $30,000 bill from my mom after the honeymoon. Needless to say, she was struggling herself. She was even working night shifts at Walmart as a manager while being a full-time teacher and mom of three! She's a freaking hero!

God bless her for all the late-night tears and angry phone calls where I was just frustrated and fed up. She had so much grace and nothing but good intentions in helping me, but she had her own money story and fears she was working through. That's when I realized I couldn't rely on someone else to help me, let alone someone who wasn't where I wanted to be. I wanted the kind of financial freedom to live an abundant life, but this was only scaring me into more poverty and scarcity.

I knew that only I could care enough about my money and financial security—no one else could do it for me. I was going to need to learn to do this on my own. I also believed deep in my soul that there had to be a better way to financial freedom than what I was being taught. Financial freedom isn't given to you; it's learned.

Boy, did I have a lot of learning and unlearning to do.

Giving Up Your Financial Power

I was recently on a phone call with my sister. She mentioned wanting to start a legacy account for her kids. I know she's been saving up for them since they were little, but this was an account to help bless them for their wedding or help them put money down on their first house. Jannette, if you are reading this, you are a saint! The way you serve and bless others through your generosity is something to be admired. I hope your kids will appreciate all you have done to provide a good life for them now and in the future.

As we got to talking, I asked what kind of account she wanted to open. She didn't really know—maybe a savings account, but she said she was going to make an appointment with her CPA. Now, I have heard my sister talk about her CPA a lot over the years.

When she needed to make some decisions on opening her business, she went to her CPA.

When we helped her get her first real estate investment property, she went to her CPA.

When she needed to get another loan to build out her location bigger because she was expanding, she called her CPA.

When she took out early retirement to buy a house, she set up a meeting with her CPA.

When she wanted to remodel her backyard, she called her CPA.

I think you are getting my point.

There is absolutely nothing wrong with having a CPA or financial advisor to seek help with your financial needs and investments. But I do believe giving them absolute authority over all the choices with your money is not just scary but leaves you powerless to grow your own financial wisdom and confidence.

For my sister, it was leaning on her CPA to make every single money decision. For you, maybe it's something or someone else.

I know I leaned super heavily on my husband to make the best decisions for us in the first few years of our investing. I remember feeling so overwhelmed when we started that I just wanted to stick my head in the sand. Heck, I would show up to the bank and sign papers for loans without ever having a conversation with Ryan about what I was signing. I would blindly trust him for years because I didn't want to feel stupid asking questions. He would chitchat back and forth with the bankers, title companies, and realtors, and I would smile and nod and act confident so no one would question me.

And before meeting Ryan, I trusted my parents. They would surely help me make the best decisions with my money. After all, they had investments, and my mom was a banker for 25 years. They knew a thing or two. Well, after accruing $120,000 in student loans and spending the only $30,000 in cash I had on books and housing, I realized maybe they weren't the best advisors for me.

But my story isn't an anomaly.

One of my all-time favorite books is called *Prince Charming Isn't Coming: How Women Get Smart About Money* by Barbara Stanny. It was after reading about her story that I decided I would never again sign a single document, loan, or investment without knowing the details of what I was signing. We even have an agreement in place that needs to be signed if I can't be at a signing.

I do this not just because it's safer and wiser for me but because I want to actually *learn*. Most men just *do*. They often jump into investing so much easier and with less caution than women. I wanted to learn the real estate game, not just be a spectator.

I wanted to know everything about our investments so I, too, could find deals and learn how to flip. So that if—God forbid—something were to happen to Ryan, I'm not totally screwed, or we lose everything we've built because I don't even know where to start with managing it. I wanted financial confidence and empowerment, and I was tired of giving that to someone else.

Prince Charming Isn't Coming really was the book that started this whole independent financial education journey for me.

In the book, Barbara Stanny shares that she married a financial advisor who, unbeknownst to her, had a gambling problem. He had her blindly signing herself into millions in debt. Her marriage ended in a divorce, where she was forced for the first time to get real about her financial future. It's an incredible story. Towards the beginning of the book, she describes what she calls the first "realization of financial enlightenment:"

"No One Will Do This for Me"
- Barbara Stanny, Prince Charming Isn't Coming

Those words hit me hard. I had to stop trusting everything and everyone in my world to figure out this money thing. I needed to wake up and stop avoiding it because I felt uncomfortable and insecure. If I was going to grow, I needed to learn the skills myself.

You are the one who is responsible for what you have and what you do with it. Now, if you are in a marriage, you both are responsible for what you have together, but that doesn't mean all the responsibility falls on one person.

A friend recently told me she doesn't really know much about their financial position or handle much of the money management in their marriage. I asked her if she had any concerns about how she would cope if something were to happen to her husband. Her response was calm but supremely naive: "There's plenty of life insurance to make sure I'm taken care of if something happens to him." So, her only fallback plan was to live off of life insurance?

Do you know what the two most common situations that force women to get their financial crap together?

Death or divorce.

Neither of these scenarios is the place where you want to make big financial decisions. Not only will the trauma of these circumstances be hard enough to go through in and of itself, but do you think we can make non-emotional choices with money when we are going through something like this?

I know someone who faced both these scenarios only ten years apart and has never been able to recover financially since—my mother. My dad died at 49 when my mom was only 47. He had a life insurance policy, but now she's nearing 68, and her only source of income is her social security check. My mom is a strong and competent woman, but she has never truly been able to recover emotionally from losing my father. She had a successful business when he was alive, but she could no longer run it after he passed. The ideas and dreams they had built together were too hard of a reminder of what she had lost to continue.

Worrying about bills and life insurance when a loved one has passed away is one of the last things you want to do. I remember when my dad died how exhausting it was to notify family, plan a funeral, and figure out when we should remove all his clothing from my mom's closet. We couldn't even remember to feed ourselves properly during the first few weeks, let alone anything else. The basic necessities of survival will stop because your whole world feels like it stops. So, the last thing you want to do in these situations is make major financial decisions.

You're going to be extremely distraught. You're gonna be in pain. These are not places where making financial decisions will come easy. There are also a lot of people who get taken advantage of in times of distress like this. They fall victim to predators, family members, or financial advisors who might want to take advantage of your lack of knowledge or your lack of preparation. You just came into some money, maybe a life insurance policy. All sorts of people will start telling you what you should do with that money.

What about a divorce? In the case of my mother, she was so distraught she walked right into an unhealthy marriage less than a year after my dad passed. Maybe she was afraid to be alone. Maybe she felt more financially secure knowing there were two incomes and reliable health insurance. Needless to say, it didn't end well.

Ryan and I have purchased more houses in foreclosure from a divorce than any other circumstance. Why did it get foreclosed on?

No one wanted to deal with it or each other, so they both stopped paying. One woman found out her husband was cheating, so she took a sledgehammer to every wall and countertop in the house. Not only did this destroy any equity they had built up in the house to split, but it ruined her credit and chances of getting another home for at least the next seven years.

It's incredibly hard to make clear, rational decisions when you are going through trauma of any type. So, let's not wait until unforeseen moments like these hit us in the face to start growing on our financial journey.

So let me ask you, are you sticking your head in the sand, assuming everyone else has your best interest in mind?

Are you solely relying on your company 401(k)?

Is your financial advisor managing your stock portfolio?

Your spouse?

Your future inheritance?

Your tax return?

Your job?

To whom or what are you giving your financial power over?

I think we all have a Prince Charming that allows us to relinquish control when we are uncomfortable, stressed, or frustrated with our financial situation. I think we all have behavioral reactions in the way we spend or save our money. You might not even be aware that you have given up your financial power.

I recently had an interesting experience with an investor and his wife. This investor has a very good-paying job that he loves. He's making great money and is making all the investment decisions for his future, his wife, and his children. He's extremely smart and feels confident in how he is providing for his family, as he should!

Because of his hard work and financial circumstances, his wife is able to stay at home, which she absolutely loves. They are happily married and have a beautiful family. One day, I asked him if his wife was involved in any of their investment decisions. His response was, "No, no, no. She doesn't even want to be a part of this. It's all above her head, and she's really not that interested."

Well, I love a good money conversation, so I asked him if he thought she would enjoy my program, where she could grow in her own financial confidence. Before I could finish, he said, "She would never do anything like that."

I was very surprised. The first time I got to have a conversation with her over dinner, I learned about her, her life, and her kids. I could tell she loved her life and was so grateful for her husband. But even though she seemingly has it all and he's provided a secure life for her and their children, she is still afraid. She told me that if anything ever happened to him, she would be screwed. She said, "I don't know where our money is. I don't know where our investments are. I don't know our accounts. I don't know what to do if he dies."

While he's worked hard to provide a secure life, she lives with all these insecurities because she is left out of all the decisions. She's not learning these skills; she's completely reliant on her husband. This was exactly what I felt ten years ago when Ryan started investing. He would run through details on investments via a quick conversation but took care of everything. Often, I just needed to sign some paperwork. I wasn't getting the education, I wasn't learning the skills, and my own competence was lacking because of it. I felt this exact same way: financially free but scared out of my mind. But we aren't the only ones. According to UBS, 56% of women married to men leave financial planning and investment decisions to their husbands.[6]

Ryan is part of a group of businessmen who focus on how to live a big life, how to be better men and/or husbands, and how to keep building wealth and the life they are after. It's been amazing to watch Ryan grow in this group. At one of their annual events, as they broke off into small groups and had discussions, he realized most of their wives were not involved in their businesses or investments. Most of their wives were completely out of the loop, not because these men were keeping things from them but because many of the wives "weren't interested." Many of the men there said the same thing: "If anything happened to me, they wouldn't know what's going on."

This raises two questions. First, how can you be building million-dollar businesses and not want security in your legacy by involving your partner? Second, why are these women not interested?

My guess is that it's not that they aren't interested; it's that it's like trying to read Greek when you only know English. I don't think these women aren't interested; I think they are overwhelmed. I think they have trouble wrapping their minds around all the details of what their husbands have built, and it's intimidating. I think many of these husbands want to provide for and protect their families, and they focus on building things that often do exactly that. Meanwhile, the things they build become a bubble that protects their wife and family but can keep her too sheltered as well. Sometimes ignorance is bliss, and if you are living a comfortable life, why ask questions? The answer to that is in what I mentioned above: Legacy.

If you want to pass on generational wealth, you can't just pass on a check. You have to pass on the education, skills, and tools to be able to multiply that check over and over. An article published by Nasdaq stated, "It is estimated that 70% of wealthy families will lose their wealth by the second generation and 90% will lose it by the third."[7] This article mentions a few reasons why this happens:

1. Generations are not taught to talk about money.
2. Prior generations worry that the next generation will become lazy or entitled.
3. Many have no clue about the value of money or how to handle it.

Sound familiar?

Do you want to build generational wealth and set the next generation up for success? Then change this! Husbands, start involving your wives in the conversations even if they seem uninterested. Wives, insert yourself in the conversations, in the rooms, at the tables where your husband does business, even if you are intimidated. Let this information bleed into your subconscious until you start feeling confident. Parents, involve your children in your money conversations and investments and share your money stories. Don't worry about them being entitled. Teach them to appreciate what you have built for them. It's time to break those generational curses once and for all.

Here's the part I want to be really clear about.

I don't want you to leave this chapter feeling guilty or beating yourself up. I don't want to do the very thing I despise the most, which is to continue to make people feel more shame and guilt about their finances.

I simply want this to be a wake-up call.

I want to see fruit and favor overflowing in your life. It starts with us owning our financial power instead of giving it to someone or something else. We have to be honest with ourselves while giving ourselves the grace we need to grow wiser each day.

We have to take control of our financial life and goals once and for all!

I made that commitment and promise to myself ten years ago, and I am still learning and growing. Success, change, and getting what you want in life doesn't happen overnight.

It happens with all the micro-commitments you make to yourself to step up and step out in faith.

It took one book for me to finally get it, and have a deep desire to take back control of my financial future. I hope this will be the book that awakens something inside of you. It took a few years for me to pay off $80,000 in my student loans, eight months to hit my first six figures in my business, and a decade of making real estate deals to become a multimillionaire, and I am not stopping there! I've started investing in stocks and crypto and am looking for more ways to grow my passive income.

I've dedicated every Monday to growing my financial IQ with something I like to call "Money Moves Monday." I block a few hours out of every Monday to read business articles and money magazines, listen to business and investing podcasts, watch Ted talks—anything I can consume to get more confident and learn more about money, business, and investing.

Don't know where to start? Sign up for my Money Moves Newsletter, which delivers financial conversations, tips, and strategies right to your inbox.

I don't know everything, but I can tell you I have come a long way. I no longer pretend to know what the bankers, lawyers, investors, and title companies all talk about. I engage them in conversations, I ask questions when I don't know something, and I feel more confident each day. In fact, most of the time now, I'm answering their questions. I want to create a movement of more empowered, financially savvy women who are ready to walk into abundance and favor. Who's coming with me?

CHAPTER 6

Every Mission Requires Money

"Money isn't everything, but everything needs money."
–Unknown

Have you ever quit your job without having another one lined up? Maybe you quit to start a business, relocate, or help a family member. You leave a known, stable source of income for something very uncertain or even nonexistent. It's really scary.

Now, imagine what Jesus would have been thinking when he quit his steady carpentry career to start his mission. Or Matthew, the rich tax collector who left a very cushy lifestyle to follow Jesus. Or Peter, who was the owner of a successful commercial fishing business. I've actually been to Peter's house in Israel, which was the biggest one on the block. He surely made a decent living for himself.

Where did Jesus and the disciples get the money to leave their jobs? Where did the resources come from to travel, eat, and pay their bills at home while they were on the road? Many of them had families, mouths to feed, and financial responsibilities that were still a priority as they spread the Gospel. How did they pay for all of this?

Wealthy women.

Luke 8 starts off by saying, *"After this, Jesus traveled about from one town and village to another, proclaiming the good news of the kingdom of God. The Twelve were with him, and also some women who had been cured of evil spirits and diseases: Mary (called Magdalene) from whom seven demons had come out; Joanna the wife of Chuza, the manager of Herod's household; Susanna; and many others. These women were helping to support them out of their own means."* (Luke 8:1-3)

This is really interesting because this minor detail didn't need to be in the Bible. It's actually kind of embarrassing to first-century male readers who didn't give much credibility to women at the time, which lends itself to the historical accuracy of this statement. If a bunch of guys were just making up this whole Jesus story, they wouldn't say women paid for everything. New Testament scholar and theologian James Dunn writes, "Such uncontrived detail indicates good tradition. Luke evidently had access here to firsthand recollections."

Sure, generous fans let Jesus and his entourage stay and eat with them for free every once in a while. But with all of the food, lodging, taxes, and supplies required for 13 people to live on the road for 2-3 years, some serious financial backing needed to be in place.

To put this in perspective, a basic meal at a traveler's inn at that time cost about a quarter of a denarius, or 25% of a normal worker's daily income. A basic meal included two pieces of meat, a chunk of bread, a bowl of lentils, and two glasses of wine. If you wanted an appetizer of 10 figs, that would cost an additional 1/8 of a denarius, or 12.5% of a daily wage. A new set of clothes cost about four denarii.[8]

And just like the exorbitant fees we pay today to live and work, like sales taxes, income taxes, road tolls, permits, entry fees, surcharges, and everything else, it would've been similar back then, too. Even though Jesus and his disciples probably did a pretty good job at keeping costs down, this mission still would've been an extremely expensive event.

Joanna, the wife of a senior Royal statesman, was probably the richest financier and would have been especially wealthy. In a time when the gap between rich and poor was already pretty extreme, she was towering in the top 1%. The disciples must've felt like they were traveling with a billionaire. Maybe they were.

As believers, many of us like to think that Jesus was super modest, poor, and didn't need much. There's nowhere explicitly in the Bible that it says that Jesus was rich or poor. But we do have studies of what it would have taken to survive financially during that time. We do know there was a financial cost that Jesus's mission required to spread the gospel and reach the nations. We know that the garments Jesus wore on the day of his crucifixion would have been valuable enough that the Roman guards gambled over them. We know the money gifted, raised, and earned would have been plentiful enough that it required Judas to manage as the treasurer.

My simple point is this: every mission requires money, even the greatest mission of all time.

The average missionary needs $30,000 to survive.[9] It costs $173,370 to run the average small church of less than 200 members.[10] The Salvation Army's annual operating budget is $3.6 Billion.[11]

Money Matters to Jesus

Money matters and our dismissal of its importance in our own personal lives and the world as a whole is just another way we justify our own lack and desire when we don't have it. There's that "Poverty Mind" again.

I can't tell you the endless times I have heard, "You shouldn't be so focused on money. There are so many more important things we should be focused on. Jesus didn't care about money."

"Jesus has more to say about finances than just about any other topic—more than the second coming, faith, prayer, and hell combined."
—Jim Baker, How Heaven Invades Your Finances

Jesus didn't question the importance and significance of the Father's provisions. The truth is that, as a believer, it should matter to us because it absolutely matters to Jesus.

There are over 2,300 verses about money, wealth, possessions, greed, money mindset, contentment, and investing. Nearly 25% of Jesus's teachings. A total of 11 of the 39 parables talk about money, and one out of every seven verses in those parables mentions money. If our churches were modeling Jesus's teachings, that would mean one out of every four weekly church services would be around the topic of money, wealth, possessions, etc.

I don't know about you, but the only two contexts in which I've ever heard the church teach about money are:

1. A sermon about not loving two masters, not storing up treasure for yourselves, the camel through a needle, or any other verse that encourages you to focus on God and not consumerism and greed. Which usually leaves us feeling like money is evil, and we should avoid it at all costs. You might spend the rest of the afternoon motivated to declutter all the extra stuff around your house and toss it in the "Goodwill donation pile."

Or

2. Every so often, there is a sermon about tithes and offerings, followed by a video on what the church has been up to with local and global missions and a special giving opportunity for an upcoming goal.

This isn't a knock on the church. I am not sure it's the church's mission to teach us about money as much as it is to teach us about Jesus. There are other resources for that. Most pastors are simply trying to teach about the character of Jesus and aren't necessarily trained on the fiscal aspects of Jesus's teachings.

But where I have struggled is when I see a huge reverence for those who sell their possessions and go on to be missionaries. We pray over them, lay our hands on them, provide them with funds, and glorify their selflessness as they walk into their season of ministry and missions. But when was the last time you saw a church do that for a businessman or woman as they got ready to sell, expand their location, or trade their business publicly? Is their mission not as important? Those funds we just donated to that missionary need to come from somewhere, right? Can they not serve in the marketplace in a way that is glorifying and honorable to God? And if we're really honest, the people who most need serving *are* in the marketplace. They're not at church.

There Are Two Points I Am Trying to Make Here

1. *Every* mission *requires* money.
2. You can serve God from the pulpit *and* the marketplace.

I want to share a story with you about a non-profit that I owned for less than a year, which I started with two of my Christian friends. It was a non-profit that funded an organization intended to counter human trafficking. We were so excited to collaborate on this mission and be able to bring awareness to this cause. We decided that we would tell stories through video and photos to reveal just how evil the human trafficking industry was and help build awareness. But instead of creating a brand-new organization, figuring out safe houses, and doing all this stuff, we decided that we would just be a pass-through organization that would fund other organizations working to prevent human trafficking and address the harms caused by it. We were so excited. I felt like God had brought us together in such a miraculous way with our talents and skills. Our first fundraiser was a huge hit.

Everything was going well; at least that's what I thought. Shortly after this fundraiser, everything started falling apart. Some conflicts arose between vision and faithfulness.

Both of the other co-founders were very creative and extremely talented. They were in charge of the video production, photography, and telling stories of these women and children in a way that shined light on the darkness of the human trafficking industry. These were their God-given gifts, and I never once doubted their abilities and talents or how God was going to use them in the organization.

My role was to run the business aspects of the organization. I set us up with articles of organization, got our 501c3 status, managed the money, and paid the bills. It might not look as fun or creative, but this is where I absolutely thrive. I love to look at P&Ls, run reports, and use my skills to increase profitability and impact. I imagine when a musician gets handed a score, the sounds come alive in their minds; they can see their hands plucking the strings, and the notes come together like the stars aligning in the sky. That's how running numbers for a business feels to me. It starts to come together in my mind, and I can instantly see opportunities and patterns. We all have our unique gifts and talents, and running this aspect of the organization was mine.

Somewhere along the way, these two co-founders approached me with concerns. My enthusiasm for the financial health of the business and the opportunities we would have to impact this cause and help fund missions was very quickly seen as "out of alignment with God's will." I was told that I wasn't trusting the Lord enough. They felt that I needed to trade managing the financial pieces of the organization with more prayer. They felt that I was so focused on the fiscal responsibility of the business that, somehow, that meant that I didn't trust God, which made me feel like my gifts were less valuable. There it was again: "You shouldn't be all about the money." But wasn't that exactly what I was hired to do? Manage the money. And if you don't know anything about running a non-profit, there are many rules you have to follow with the government to maintain your 501c3 status. But instead of utilizing my skills, I was told I just needed to trust God more. That's like telling them not to worry about putting a memory card in the camera: "Just trust God. If it's His will, He will make sure it's in the camera when the time is right."

Or it might also have nothing to do with God's will and everything to do with just checking the camera. Or maybe—stay with me here—God's will *is* for you to check the camera. Now that's deep. I think you get the point I am trying to make.

I know this story isn't unique either. There have been so many times when I've had conversations with church leaders about money and business, and I felt the same sentiment: like I shouldn't care about money, that I'm too focused on the money, that I'm not trusting in God. It was confusing because while I didn't have the skills to create beautiful videos and storytelling, I did have the skills to manage a business and raise money that made a large difference. Was that not also serving the mission? Were these not also gifts from the Lord?

Why do I feel like an outcast when I talk about money, business, or success? If I talk about money these days, it gets categorized as "prosperity gospel." I get shunned and constantly feel the need to overcompensate and prove that I do, in fact, love Jesus more than money. Why is that?

The point in sharing this story is that somewhere in the church, we have decided that poverty and giving up your possessions are virtuous. But the moment that you have someone successful, well-off, and who has material possessions, somehow they aren't serving God and only serving themselves. But can't it also be true that they are stewarding their skills, talents, and abilities wisely, that God is blessing and multiplying those efforts, which is then, in turn, creating more provisions? And doesn't the Bible also say, "Do not compare your lot to others?" Who are we to judge God's blessings on one person's life or compare them to someone else's?

Who are we to determine someone's heart or intentions?

During the time that the organization was running, there was an opportunity to go to Iraq and film a documentary on ISIS refugees with another organization. My husband was asked to go with one of our co-founders, not just because he was skilled and had a degree in film production. The only other person who could go was married to the other founder who was going, and if something had happened to both of them on this trip, their kids would become orphans. To say it was a dangerous and serious mission would be an understatement. It took us three seconds to decide that Ryan was going to go with her, and I was incredibly proud of him. We all knew the risks involved and trusted that God would protect them even as we were being called into the darkest of places.

On this mission, they were going to go to these refugee camps. The aim was to tell the stories of families and victims who'd been affected by ISIS. People had family members who were taken from them and were now sex slaves to this terrorist organization.

It was one of the scariest weeks of my life. It was a very covert operation, and Ryan wasn't allowed access to a cell phone. I didn't know where he would be. It was a very secretive mission with several former CIA agents and Navy SEALS. But I knew God had a major purpose for Ryan and this co-founder to tell these stories so that we could share them with the world and make a difference.

This experience was transformative for my husband, Ryan. Up to this point, he had never been on a mission trip and this one was so sensitive. The stories they accessed were so heartbreaking and unfathomable. The documentary they filmed was beautiful, but the content they shared is the type that haunts you for the rest of your life.

Ryan had one goal: to focus on filming and capturing the lives of these refugees. He had no idea just how profound this mission would be. You see, it wasn't just the stories that motivated him, but something else he witnessed that would change his life forever.

Many of these families that were in this refugee camp had escaped ISIS but had daughters who were taken hostage as sex slaves. They wept at the thought of their daughter and the horrors she was facing. As a Christian, you might feel called to pray with them and lay your hands on them, but this couldn't be further from what they wanted at that moment. I'm not devaluing the power of prayer, but let me explain.

These families had been removed from their homes and cities, and family members were killed, raped, and sold at the hands of ISIS and their radical religious beliefs. These refugees didn't know Jesus. Laying hands on them and praying to another God they did not know or believe in their time of need would have made us appear no better than the very people they were running from.

Again, don't get me wrong here. Prayer is extremely powerful and necessary, but in this particular circumstance, it wasn't what these people would have wanted. Visibly praying over them would have also put a target on the team's backs and put all their lives at risk, too. While all the people on this mission were undoubtedly praying in their hearts, they were strongly advised against doing so in any visible way inside these refugee camps, and I am sure you have an understanding now of why.

But there was one way that they could show love and care, and that they didn't just want to exploit their stories or convert them: money.

Handing them cold, hard cash was the thing that showed them love because it allowed them to buy the very thing they needed: their daughter back. Ryan and this entire group would be in a tent and lay out a row of $100 bills in front of a family who now had hope they could bring their daughter home. They could buy their daughter's freedom and rescue her from human trafficking. They were overjoyed because the money desperately mattered to them.

Do our prayers matter? Without a doubt. But how did you think these people would feel—these people who didn't know God, who were seeing ISIS kill for theirs—the moment someone met their most fundamental needs? They felt loved because of the provisions that were provided and the real needs that were being met—in this case, through money. This is exactly what Jesus told us to do—give one's wealth to the poor, oppressed, and the needy.

Ryan was able to see an up-close experience where money and the stewardship of that money meant everything. Were he and this group supposed to just go to their rooms, pray to themselves, and hope God would take care of everything, or were they the very answer to their prayers while also showing worship and faithfulness in their giving?

We all know money matters. It's what our churches need to run; it's what your favorite non-profit needs to finance its mission; it's what the homeless ask for to pay for food; it's what keeps a roof over most of our heads. And as you learned in a previous chapter, money isn't inherently bad. Some people like to think money is just a figment of our imagination but try explaining that to your landlord on rent day.

It's easy to judge something you don't have much of, and it's easy to envy that which someone else has. It's easy to pass judgment on what others do with their money and assume the worst. How many times have you sat in a church service and wondered if they needed those extra lights or surround sound speakers? These thoughts and judgments are rooted in sin and are all examples of the "Poverty Mind."

The quicker you stop looking outward and start looking inward in your own heart, the more likely it is that you will be able to see how God can and will use you and your finances for His Kingdom. God is ultimately in control, but that doesn't mean we should never use the experiences, skills, and opportunities He has given us and instead sit on our hands waiting. It doesn't mean one person's calling or Kingdom assignment is better than anyone else's. We are called to different places and have unique experiences God has shaped us through so that we can serve Him in every aspect of our lives, including our finances!

Funny enough, after we closed the non-profit, one of the co-founders started a new one right where we left off. Same annual fundraiser, a different name, and years later she would approach me to ask if she could hire me to run the financial aspects of this new organization. I couldn't help but laugh at the irony. Turns out that being fiscally responsible is something that was deemed important and worthy of the cause. I politely declined.

The point of this story is to emphasize that money actually matters. Money can save lives. Money can provide water wells. Money can buy women and children out of sex slavery. Money can support the missions and missionaries. Every single mission requires money.

Even Jesus's Mission Required Money

On a recent trip to Israel, I had the privilege of being able to go on a pilgrimage. Israel is not a very large country, so I started to get a sense of the distance of these towns mentioned in the Bible and how long it would have taken to walk from Nazareth to the Sea of Galilee. It really gave you an idea of what it would have been like to live in these cities and what experiences Jesus would be having. From the baths, temples, and everything in between, you just got a feel for the everyday life Jesus would have lived. Jesus experienced everything it was to be human. He wasn't immune to pain, suffering, and heartbreak. Likewise, Jesus was no exception to having to get a job, earn wages, and meet the requirements that came along with Roman and Jewish taxes.

Think about that for a second. The Son of God still had to pay taxes. Do you think the Romans made an exception for Jesus?

In Matthew 17:24-27, after Jesus and his disciples arrived in Capernaum, the collectors of the two-drachma tax came to Peter and asked, *"Doesn't your teacher pay the temple tax?"* Peter replied that he did.

Jesus would have needed to pay taxes and regular expenses like food, just like the rest of society. There was no exception, even for God Himself. In fact, for most of Jesus's life, He was a carpenter in the marketplace. He helped run the family business.

Jesus didn't ignore His responsibilities for the everyday cost of living, food, and daily essentials. He made products and sold them to help pay for these things. He didn't ignore the importance of money and its role in society, and He is God!

We know Joseph had his business for quite some time. It must have been successful enough to pass on to his sons. Joseph had built a legacy and quite a reputation, to the point where townsfolk even called Jesus "the craftsman's son."

I can't imagine the Son of God creating anything with low standards. Could you imagine Jesus creating something cheap like Ikea that feels like it's going to fall apart in five seconds? No, Jesus didn't cut corners. He didn't overlook the importance of utilizing His skills, His talents, and His craftsmanship, even though He knew He had a bigger purpose in life. Even though He was God, He would end up giving His life for us. He didn't ignore the importance of the marketplace or the importance of money to operate a business and fund His lifestyle.

We're not supposed to love money or desire wealth over God. That's what we are continually reminded of throughout the scriptures.

Money is simply a tool that can do a lot of incredible things. It's a tool to pay for the costs of building a well to provide clean water. It's a tool that every organization needs to serve its mission in our communities. If there is a calling and a mission in your heart, it likely requires money for you to fulfill it.

Even if you want to dedicate your entire life to going to some remote village, serving in that village, and spreading the gospel, you'll still need funding. You'll still need to figure out how to have the basic necessities in life, which will require money. And you know where it's going to come from? The people in the marketplace who are making it who want to support your mission, church, or organization.

This is where missions rely on the marketplace. This means the money you make at your job or the income you make in your small business—your hair salon, your retail store, your dry cleaning business—all have the ability to not only generate income to keep your business alive and provide you with personal provisions but can be the very vehicle that produces the money to help fund the causes that fuel these missions.

There's not a single cause in the world that couldn't use money to help solve a real problem and a real solution. So when we remove the significance of money and dismiss its importance because we just feel uncomfortable with it or because we think it's wrong, we're dismissing its value and how God can and will use what He blesses us with to be able to make an incredible difference in our world.

Money isn't the key to our salvation or eternal happiness, but it's pretty helpful here on Earth.

CHAPTER 7

Men, Marriage, and Money

"I can live without money, but I cannot live without love."
–Judy Garland

I felt it necessary to write an entire chapter around the topic of marriage and money. Not only because financial problems contribute to 20%–40% of divorces but because managing money by yourself is one thing; managing it with another person who also has their own habits, money stories, and money beliefs adds a new level of challenge. Marriages face specific challenges when you combine your incomes and expenses, set your financial goals, and share your dreams and ambitions in life. All of which usually require this one simple tool: money.

If you aren't yet married but plan to be, stick around. There are some invaluable lessons to learn on this topic to be better prepared and lay the foundation for a healthy shared "money life" with your future partner.

I read a lot of books on the topic of marriage and money. Many of them still advise separating your money and your bank accounts and protecting your own interest at all costs. I haven't found a lot of information out there on how to work together and be unified and see your marriage as not simply a financial transaction but the incredible union God intended marriage to be. Where are the books on faith and finances for married couples? There are more resources and discussions out there for couples around the topic of our sex lives, but what about our money lives? Maybe that will be the next book I write because as I dove into the topic of marriage and money, it felt way too divisive and discouraging.

After Jesus, the topic I most like learning and reading about is money, so when I found out that my favorite shark, Kevin O'Leary, wrote a book called *Cold Hard Truth on Men, Women, and Money*, I couldn't wait to get my hands on it. I devoured it in one day. There was some valuable information inside, but by the time I finished, I felt like I'd been punched in the gut.

Of course, there was the same old "cut out your coffee" speech, which honestly is like beating a dead horse at this point. I sigh even as I write this because it's exhausting to feel like I'm fighting this narrative in every book I pick up. Listen, I really respect Kevin O'Leary, and he has some great advice. I love his YouTube channel and his no-BS approach. I also know he loves fine watches and owns some of the most expensive specimens on the market; his collection is worth $3,000,000. When he travels, he carries 17 to 20 of these pieces with him, which requires hiring a certain level of security. If I were sitting with him in an interview, I would ask this one question: "How was it that you were able to have the self-discipline to save $5 every day by skipping your latte, and how integral was skipping your coffee in helping you invest in businesses, achieve massive success, and a net worth of $400 million?"

I bet he didn't get those watches by skipping coffee, and no one is telling him to cut back on the watches because they aren't necessary. I'm sure, in the beginning, he made many sacrifices to get where he is today. All success requires sacrifice, but he's not looking back on the good ol' days when he made his coffee at home. At some point, there was a shift. He took a leap—likely a big risk. Most successful people have a "risked it all" moment in their journey to success because true success isn't made by saving $5 on a latte. It's made by increasing your income through business and investments. I just wish that was emphasized more than dwelling on this one specific expense.

Ok, rant over; let's get back to his chapter on marriage and money. Not only is he an advocate for keeping your money separate, but he also recommends keeping your savings and investments a secret from your spouse. He discourages marriage completely if you don't plan on having children. He encourages you to live together and be life partners, but no kids, no marriage. We know from a biblical perspective what is broken here, but the real kicker for me was in these next few sentences, "I'll add this bit of atypical advice: If my potential partner carried a lot of debt, I'd delay the wedding until the debt was gone, or consider marrying someone else."

I'll admit this one felt a little personal and hit home. I had never thought about what my life would have looked like if Ryan had rejected me because of my student loan debt. It actually brought tears to my eyes. What would my life look like if Ryan followed that advice? First of all, if I was making all my payments on my student loans and following the terms in place, I would literally still be paying those debts off today. That means I would be unable to take a husband until I was 43 years old because a standard term on a student loan is 20 years. I would need to forego marriage and potentially children, all because I carried too much debt.

Secondly, I already had to go through so much anguish, doubt, fear, and guilt associated with my student loans. To begin with, I was encouraged to go to college and take out loans to ensure a good job and future. Then, when I do this and accumulate debt, I am like the plague and need to be avoided at all costs. There was so much shame involved in taking the typical advice, but I didn't understand where I went wrong. I was already emotionally stressed that I was the one bringing so much debt into our marriage. I felt an incredible amount of guilt, but I can't imagine how much worse this would have been if there had been a contingency in our marriage. I can't imagine Ryan being like, "Sorry, I can't marry you until your debt is paid off."

And if I'm following all the advice that "they" give you—cut up all my credit cards, focus on my debt, pay off $120,000 on my loans—I'm not gonna be getting married for the next 10, 15, or 20 years.

So, how much money do I need in my account for my future husband to find me valuable or worthy of marriage?

Even as I scroll through social media, some of the topics being discussed are whether you should ask for copies of a man's bank accounts before you go on your first date. There was one woman who went around her city posting signs that said, "I'm looking for my rich husband. Call me if you qualify."

I don't believe that money or lack of it should be a primary reason you get married to someone in the first place. If that was the case, Ryan and I would never have done so. We were both broke and didn't have any financial security to offer each other. If I can't provide for him and he can't provide for me, should we just find other people? No, it's horrible advice! This idea that you will have financial security if you marry the right person is quite the gamble. Money comes and goes, and the false sense of security we put on our significant other to protect us is easily tested by sudden hardships and unexpected death. Nothing is permanent. Our trust should be only in the Lord to provide and protect. It is possible to grow with your partner and learn. And from my experience, it's a heck of a lot easier when you work together as a team.

I'm not saying you shouldn't care about the financial health of your potential life partner and have important discussions before committing to a marriage, but somewhere along the way, our society lost sight of the heart of the person, not their bank account or monetary value. God didn't create marriage for financial gain.

Marriage is not a financial contract; it's a covenant.

It's intended to reflect the love and relationship between Christ and His Church. God designed marriage for partnership, spiritual intimacy, and the ability to pursue God—together.[12]

In Genesis 2:23, Adam proclaims, *"This is the flesh of my flesh and bone of my bone... therefore a man shall leave his father and his mother and hold fast to his wife, and they shall become one flesh."*

When you marry someone, you become one flesh. You are a unit, you are spiritually intertwined, you are one. It doesn't say, "You are one, except with money. Keep that separate."

I get it, though. I know it's difficult to be on the same page with money. I know you might have different goals when it comes to your finances. You or your partner might feel different fears and insecurities around money. You likely came from different financial backgrounds, and sometimes, it feels like you won't ever be on the same page. But we have to understand that in addition to having different money influences, men and women are simply wired differently.

We're both made in the same image, we're both made by the same Creator, but we have differences in our behaviors, emotions, and how our brains are wired. Now, I don't want you to think this is one of those radical feminist books where I'm going to bash men, blame them for our oppression, and try to convince you that men are the enemy. I love men. In a world that continues to pit us against each other, I cling to knowing our Creator knew what he was doing when He put us both on this planet. We have different strengths, desires, and behaviors, which I think are beautiful—albeit sometimes frustrating, too. I like to think God has a sense of humor, and in making us different, He helps us be more patient and introspective. He uses these differences to help us grow closer to each other and to Him.

For the sake of this book, I simply want to recognize the beautiful differences that we have, and specifically the different ways that we approach money.

Understanding each other, learning to communicate with each other, and learning how each other's fears come up, patterns, and spending habits will all help create a more successful, sustainable, and loving marriage.

Men are uniquely wired to protect and provide for their families. That doesn't mean that they are the sole income earner or the breadwinner. It simply means that they want to protect and provide the things that are most important to them, which are their family, their wife, their kids, and the next generation. It's a huge need.

Ed Silvoso wrote in *Women: God's Secret Weapon*, "Men are designed to be protectors and providers. Failure to be either creates a void right at the centers of their identity."

Whereas women also have desires to provide and protect, they tend to look outside of their own family unit and find empowerment in helping others. "A large body of evidence suggests that women are often more prosocial (for example, generous, altruistic and inequality averse) than men." A study published in *Nature Human Behavior* found that in women, part of the brain showed a greater response when sharing money. Meanwhile, in men, the same structure showed more activity when they kept the cash for themselves.[13] As Philippe Tobler, co-author of the new study, sees it, "Women put more subjective value on prosocial behavior, and men find selfish behavior more valuable."[14]

This doesn't mean one is right or wrong or better than the other; it simply shows the different drivers, motivators, and experiences men and women have around money. In the decade of helping female entrepreneurs, I have noticed this pattern. Women see success and money as a way to contribute. Men tend to see success and money as a challenge. It's something they want to achieve or conquer, where success, wealth, and financial freedom become a scorecard. What I've noticed from working with thousands of women is that it's usually way less about a scorecard and a way to measure up against others and more of a vehicle or way to serve others.

It might be at her own expense, too. She will give the shirt off her back or the change in her pocket even if she's behind on her own bills. She will go to great lengths to help others. I've seen it countless times. She will start a business even if it doesn't make her any money because she wants to help others and provide something for the community. She rarely starts the business for the money in the first place. Many times, she will not pay herself for years as long as she knows she has provided a paycheck for her employees.

She might be down in sales, but she's still going to say yes to a box of cookies from the Girl Scouts or sponsoring the Little League team because she genuinely cares about the well-being of the community as a whole, and she feels a deep sense of connection when she can contribute her resources and her time, even if it's at her own expense.

Does any of this sound familiar? Again, there are obviously men who give back and care about others. We are complicated humans, and I'm not interested in putting anyone in a box, but in over a decade of working with thousands of female entrepreneurs (and hundreds of men, too), I've noticed some differences in what motivates us when it comes to creating wealth.

I think there's something really beautiful about the way that we are all created, and the ways we complement each other. I truly believe we are most powerful when we work together. We have a lot to contribute and can create amazing things through our gifts and our resources, our time, and our money. My hope is that we learn more about each other and these behaviors so we can work together to become amazing stewards of God's wealth.

Money Mistakes to Avoid Before You Get Married

If you are single and reading this book, and you aspire to get married one day, I want to share what I've learned. This is the kind of money conversation I wish someone would have had with me before I got married.

If you are already married, it's not too late to implement some of these tips to help improve and strengthen your marriage. My husband Ryan and I haven't argued about money in over a decade. We have a healthy relationship that is God-centered, respectful, and completely comfortable talking about our "money life" in ways most couples avoid altogether.

It wasn't always this way. During our first years of marriage, I used to cry every time budgets and money were brought up. I felt tremendously guilty for the debt I was bringing into our marriage when Ryan had zero debt coming into our relationship. We even faced near bankruptcy together in our second year of marriage, which we are both convinced would have ended in divorce for the majority of people. It was excruciating. We've built businesses together, closed them together, and faced a lot of trials and tests of faith with our finances. We aren't perfect by any means, but we have learned a lot in our 15-year relationship and have implemented some key elements that have allowed us to thrive together in our faith and finances through any and all storms. My hope is that you, your spouse, or your future spouse never argue about money again. That you find strength in working together and that the topic of money becomes one you enjoy discussing and working toward together.

I've put together a list of common money marriage mistakes to avoid in hopes that we can break through the uncomfortable conversations and build firm foundations in all areas of our relationships, which include money.

Mistake #1: Not Having Money Conversations

A report by Edelman Financial Engines stated that only 37% of couples had detailed discussions about their financial goals, and only 38% talked about the actual ins and outs of their finances.[15]

We need to be able to have simple, ordinary conversations around money—not arguments. They don't need to be heated, angry, or, as I like to say, "passionate." I'm Italian, so my volume tends to be in the higher range. I'm talking about normal conversations when you casually ask someone, "What have they been up to lately?" but instead, it's, "What is your current credit score?" See, it's easy.

Before getting married, it's important to have open and honest conversations about money. You need to be on the same page. When things get tough or you get stressed (and you will), just remember you are on the same team. The leading cause of divorce isn't the actual money struggles; it's not having the same goals with your money.

I can tell you from experience it is way easier to work together than against each other. You can accelerate much faster when you work together.

There is a lot less resentment or stress put on one partner when you work together.

I can't stress enough the importance of having these conversations before you commit to a marriage together. I would encourage you to speak with a mentor, do premarital counseling, and seek financial advice from people you look up to and who have a healthy marriage. Ask them how they manage their money together and get some pointers. Here are some questions to consider asking your partner as you start to get more serious in your relationship. And be sure to approach these out of love and compassion, not interrogation:

What is your current financial situation?
- Do you have any debt?
- What's your credit score?
- Do you have any assets or money saved up?

What are your career plans?
- How much money do you make in your current career?
- Where do you see yourself professionally in the next five years?
- What kind of money do you want to make in your career?

What are your spending habits?
- Are you a spender or a saver?
- How do you budget for your expenses?
- What were your experiences with money growing up?

How should we manage our finances together?
- Should we have joint or separate bank accounts?
- Who will be responsible for managing the bills?
- How do we make purchasing decisions together?
- Should we have a limit for individual spending or discuss all purchases together?

- How will we save and plan for big expenses?
- Do you believe in giving to charity or tithing? What causes or organizations are important to you?
- How do you handle financial stress or disagreements?

What are your long-term financial goals?
- What are your savings goals?
- Are you interested in investing?
- What does retirement look like to you?
- Where do you stand with taking financial risks?

What is your attitude towards debt?
- How do you feel about debt?
- What is your ideal strategy for paying off existing or future debt?
- Do you believe in using credit cards regularly?

What are your views on children and finances?
- Do you want children, and if so, how many?
- Do you want our kids to go to private school, public school, or be homeschooled?
- What are your thoughts on allowances, teaching kids about money, etc.?

These are basic questions and conversations that need to happen before you can ever think about starting a life together. These conversations should be approached with an open heart, empathy, understanding, and—most importantly—without judgment. Remember, we all have money stories and influences, so it's important to have grace with one another. Conversely, though, you can't simply avoid these questions because they are uncomfortable or you are so deeply in love that nothing else could possibly matter.

So many times when you're in love, you get swept up. You're super excited because you've met the love of your life, and nothing else matters, and you feel like you're suddenly in a romantic movie. I felt like that, too. I met my dream man, and it felt like a fairy tale—until reality set in. I left my job and moved across the country to a place where I didn't know a single person. We got engaged, and we were broke, trying to figure out how we could have a wedding when we had less than $2,000 in our bank account. We bought our first house together, started paying a mortgage, combined bills, and bought our first rental property together.

You start to realize it's not just you anymore. Your spending habits affect someone else. You can't just wing it anymore. You can't go buy whatever you want because now you have to consider someone else. You need to know you will be compatible with your money by having these basic conversations with each other from the moment your relationship starts to get serious.

If Ryan and I were not on the same page about core fundamental values around our faith, our goals, and our money, we wouldn't have gotten married. That's not to say all these things had to be perfectly aligned or that we had to have everything in order for us to consider marriage. I don't think that is realistic. But we did need to know where we were and where we wanted to go in life to be able to see if the relationship would work.

If you have these foundational components of your life that do not match up, it's going to collide at some point in your marriage. There's going to be resentment, there's going to be anger, there's going to be the need to feel like you have to change someone. And this is completely unfair because you married someone for who they are, not who you want them to be.

Those conversations need to continue throughout your marriage. You're going to have times when money stressors come up, or unexpected expenses come up, that cause strain on the relationship. Your goals are going to change. Your money stories and influencers will come out. Your needs and desires will evolve. So if you can start the foundation of your relationship around having conversations, you'll be able to address these things quickly when they arise, and without so much heightened emotion around them.

Mistake #2: Not Discussing a Prenup

This is one topic where I see a lot of people get super offended, but let me explain. I'd happily bet money that there aren't a whole lot of people who stand at the altar and think they are ever going to divorce the person to whom they are getting ready to say, "I do." I don't think most people get into a marriage just to get a divorce. I bet most people believe this is going to be their person for life. But the cold, hard truth is that many marriages will end in divorce, and divorce can be devastating financially.

Let's get the basics here.

What is a prenup?

A prenup, or prenuptial agreement, is an agreement made by a couple before they get married that clarifies the ownership of their respective assets in the case that the marriage fails.

What exactly does a prenup do?

The prenup typically lists each person's assets and debts and explains how the couple wants to handle these should they divorce in the future.

Why would you want a prenup?

To protect your assets.

What happens if you don't get a prenup?

In the case you do get a divorce, you leave it up to a family law judge to determine how to split your assets. In the U.S., most states follow common law, so once you are married all your accounts, assets, and debts are divided in half in a divorce, regardless of whether you have separate accounts or you are the main account holder. This would include your debts, credit cards, and retirement accounts as well.

Who should get a prenup?
Anyone with substantial assets entering into a marriage.

It's important to consider what you have coming into a marriage. Do you own properties? Do you own a business, or do you have a business partner? Maybe this is your second marriage, and you have a large retirement account that has accrued, along with a house and children, from your previous marriage. You will want to get a prenup if you want your assets to go to your children and not your new spouse. Without this or other types of future planning like a will or trust, most states will divide your assets between you and your spouse in the case of a divorce.

Ryan and I never got a prenup because when we got married, we were broke and didn't own anything. We didn't have any money, which made it pretty easy. I had my student loan debt, so I put in place a life insurance policy that would cover my six figures of debt should something happen to me, so he would not be personally responsible. That was it.

If Ryan and I were to meet now, with the wealth and assets we currently have, we would view the prenup strictly as an insurance policy. We wouldn't have any intentions to divorce, but a prenup is in place just in case the worst should happen.

Moral of the story: there's a time and a place to get a prenup. It's not emotional. It doesn't mean your future spouse doesn't love you. Some people perceive prenups negatively as indicating that people aren't fully committed to the marriage or they don't trust their partner. It may feel like they have one foot out the door, but that's simply not the case. Both parties should consider their assets and create a future plan by using a prenup when appropriate. As they say, the only people who win in court are the lawyers, so any measures that can help you avoid it are likely to be beneficial.

Mistake #3: Going into Debt for Your Wedding

Do not, I repeat, do not get into debt for your wedding. It's not worth it. Don't start your life together by adding extra strain on your marriage. When you get married and start a new life, there are so many other challenges you will face, like living together, sharing closets, changing your name, planning your family, and so on. The last thing you need is to add one more financial stressor to your life.

If you have the money, and it doesn't require you to go into debt, by all means, have the wedding of your dreams. Why should my personal experience or my own financial lack impact your wedding choices? But if you are reading this book, you likely aren't rolling in the kind of money that's going to buy you a grand wedding.

In 2022, the average wedding in the U.S. cost $30,000.[16] According to the United States Census Bureau, in 2022, the median age for marriage was approximately 28–30 years old.[17] According to the Federal Reserve, the median savings for 30-year-olds is $5,400.[18] A 2018 survey from Student Loan Hero reported that 74% of couples planned to go into debt for their weddings.[19]

And it's not just couples that are affected financially by weddings. According to the newest LendingTree survey of nearly 2,000 U.S. consumers, 40% of those who've attended a wedding in the past five years have gone into debt to be there. For those who've been part of a bridal party, that percentage jumps to a staggering 62%.[20]

Why? Why are we doing this? Celebrating the union of a couple who commits to each other for life is a beautiful thing, but harming yourself, your guests, and your family to celebrate is a difficult pill to swallow.

I remember when Ryan and I were engaged. I was so excited to start planning our wedding, but deep down, I knew it would be nearly impossible for us to have a "normal" wedding. Combined, we had a few thousand dollars in our names, which was barely enough to pay our bills and rent. Neither one of us came from a super wealthy family, so we knew we were probably on our own. My sister, in all her excitement, sent me a few books on wedding etiquette, budgets, and planning your dream wedding. I remember getting a few pages into one of the books. It talked about which side of the family pays for the rehearsal dinner and that the bride's family would bear the majority of the wedding expenses. I flipped through a few pages that detailed how many layers the wedding invitations should be between the invitation, matching return envelopes, and RSVP cards with dinner selections, and I immediately felt overwhelmed. I looked up at Ryan with tears in my eyes. I knew my family didn't have the money to pay for our wedding.

I had never thought about my wedding, what it would be like, or daydreamed about my wedding as a kid. I knew I wanted something different than the typical wedding, and at the time, I had only been to a few weddings, including being the maid of honor for my sister's 500-guest wedding. All I really remember of that wedding was seeing my sister and her new husband go from table to table, greeting everyone and thanking them for coming. I don't remember watching them dance outside of the first dance or sitting down to eat, and I don't even think they got a single piece of the five-tiered wedding cake she spent so much time picking out and taste-testing. They diligently went to each table for hours, which to me seemed miserable. It didn't look fun. Years later, I found out that they had spent over $30,000 on that wedding, an astronomical amount back in 1998. Today that would be almost $58,000![21]

Now, it was my turn. I knew they spent years paying off that debt. I watched my sister struggle on food stamps and moonlighting as a manager at Walmart after she graduated college. I was already six figures in student loan debt, so the thought of taking on more debt devastated me. I had a choice at that moment, and it was an easy one. I threw every single book in the garbage. Nope, I wasn't falling for keeping up with "the Joneses" or trusting what "they" say anymore.

Ryan and I were going to have a wedding, but it was going to be on our terms. I called my mom to see if she had saved any money for our wedding.

(This was never an assumption, by the way, nor do I consider it a requirement.) She told me she had $5,000 she would like to give us for the event. Can you guess what our entire budget was for our wedding? That's right, $5,000 because if you haven't picked up on it yet, Ryan and I had very little money, and we were basically living paycheck to paycheck. I was thrilled and incredibly grateful to have anything. Ryan and I were used to getting scrappy and figuring things out on a budget. This was our time to shine. With a little creativity, some DIY projects, and the help of our generous friends and family, not only were we able to pull off the wedding of our dreams, but we were also able to go on an all-expenses-paid honeymoon that is still one of the greatest trips of our lives. Our $5,000 wedding was featured in *Montana Bride* magazine, and I can guarantee ours was the most inexpensive wedding in the entire issue. The best part was that it was fun; we enjoyed every single minute, and our guests still talk about the epic carnival wedding they attended.

I won't bore you with the details of our wedding, but I will share a few tips to help you avoid going into debt for your wedding.

1. **Get creative.** Who says you have to follow any rules and etiquette? Your wedding should embody who you two are. Ryan and I are like children at heart. We build forts in our living room on date night, and our decision to have a carnival wedding was because we love games and rides. Dancing and three-course dinners weren't for us. It is your wedding, after all, you should enjoy it to the fullest!
2. **Forego the target gift registry.** Set up a honeymoon registry instead, where your guests can contribute to a vacation and experiences. Gift registries fill up your home with stuff you likely don't need. Creating memories is the best thing money can buy and you will remember it so much more than the toaster someone got you.
3. **Cut the guest list.** If you don't know your great-aunt, Susie, Jonny, your third cousin twice removed, or your mom wants you to invite every babysitter who ever watched you, they don't need to be at the

wedding. I remember my mother emailing me a long list of people I had to invite. I politely declined. It's your wedding, and you don't owe it to anyone but yourself and your future husband or wife to spend it enjoying your time together and with those you truly want to celebrate with.

4. **Have a destination wedding.** This is an easy way to cut the guest list and save on extra mouths to feed. There are some incredible all-inclusive destinations that can also double as your honeymoon. Your family and guests will likely have a better time too. Might as well get a vacation out of the deal.

5. **Keep your wedding party small.** Unless you can afford to accommodate your wedding party, don't put them through the financial hardships of destination bachelorette and bachelor parties, paying for their awful bridesmaid dresses they most certainly will never wear again, and on top of that, expect them to learn a dance in their free time that's perfectly timed and rehearsed to make sure it gets you the 10 seconds of wedding footage you hope to go viral. The bigger the bridal party, the more stress. Trust me; I owned a wedding venue and helped a lot of brides fight back tears while their bridal party drank free booze and disappeared when the bride needed help to pee.

6. **Skip the expensive venue!** This will be one of your biggest expenses, and there are so many ways around this. We rented out the entire Thomas Carnival the night before it opened to the public. Yes, our guests got to ride a full-size Ferris Wheel, the Zipper, a merry-go-round, and play carnival games. It looked extremely expensive, but without going into all the details, we got the entire thing for free. It was absolutely a miracle from God. I think they thought it was so cool and felt honored that we wanted to celebrate at their venue. Also, get married on Monday through Thursday, and you will pay a

fraction of the price. At my wedding venue, we had special prices for weekday weddings and welcomed them anytime.

Following these tips will save you thousands of dollars. If we are following "Girl Math," it's like you just made $5,000+ dollars reading this book. Too soon, lol? In all seriousness, be willing to be flexible and not go into debt for your wedding. I'm not saying your wedding isn't important, but it can be everything you have ever imagined, and you don't have to harm your financial future to do it. I'm living proof!

Mistake #4: Not Having Regular Scheduled Monthly Money Meetings

Nearly eight years ago, Ryan and I began having dedicated monthly money meetings. They changed the way we made and managed money together. This is where we set goals, talk about work and our future, and discuss various investments, business opportunities, challenges, and setbacks.

We do not discuss housework, such as who needs to run to the grocery store this week, if the dogs have been fed, etc. We keep these meetings focused on one thing: our financial growth. We will update each other on our business income and expenses. We will talk about current investments and future projects. These are scheduled monthly in our calendars, and we often have them outside of the comfort of our home. We like to book a meeting room, go to a coffee shop, and sometimes lunch, but somewhere where we can stay focused and communicate with each other like we are in a board meeting with a business partner. We find that leaving our house and having these discussions in a public space changes the way we talk to each other. We tend to talk to our spouses a little bit differently than our co-workers, employees, or potential business partners. By having this change of environment and setting a specific expectation, we are able to have smoother conversations where negative emotions are kept more at bay. It helps us to have more calm, logical communication and to set common goals.

This is where you should be able to tell your spouse your current fears, desires, needs, and leave nothing off the table. It's important to come into these meetings knowing you are a team. You both have the best intentions and want to work on building your abundant life together. That's what these meetings allow you to do.

Maybe you are reading this and can't imagine this would work for you and your spouse. *There's no way they would be open to these conversations,* you tell yourself. Every time you try to talk about money before, it ends up in a fight. Don't be discouraged. I believe God wants to transform and restore all areas of your life. Why would your money be any different? Lift this fear and doubt in prayer and have faith. It might feel a bit weird at first and maybe even a little awkward, but just like anything, it takes practice.

Eventually, you both might just come to love these meetings and leave feeling empowered. We like to start and end these meetings with prayer. Invite God into your "money life." Ask for provisions, protection, and guidance with your money. Ask for opportunities to steward money in a way that honors Him and His plans above all. Don't be afraid: He already knows the desires of your heart.

I've coached many couples who have implemented these meetings, and it's been incredible to see the shift in how they work together and honor each other in this area of their relationship. If the very thing that splits people up is money, wouldn't it be a good decision to dedicate time to growing together here, too? Test it out. I dare you! Then, share with me your breakdowns and breakthroughs because I can't wait to see how God transforms your money lives together.

It's not always easy or comfortable, but staying where you are isn't getting you where you want to go. When Ryan and I had these meetings early on, I would share how scared I was to invest in real estate and how I wasn't as risk-tolerant as he was. I was vulnerable, and you know what happened? I learned he was scared, too.

He had his own set of fears: fear of failure, fear that he'd make the wrong decision on a property, fear that something wouldn't go as planned, or that it would turn out to be a bad investment. I was relieved because I thought I was the only one feeling this way. These meetings helped us meet each other where we were and encouraged us both to move past the fear and become more united and stronger together.

You have to work together with your spouse, not against each other. This doesn't mean your goals have to be the same or perfectly aligned all the time. I like to think of it as if we are a couple of trains. Our trains might be on the same track; other times, they are parallel to each other. Every once in a while the tracks come together and connect with another track. There are times when you and your significant other will be hitched together with similar goals, and other times that it might feel like you are on completely different tracks, but that doesn't mean you aren't heading toward the same destination. These meetings are to help ensure you both don't derail.

Set these monthly meetings to talk about your goals, your future, different investments you want to try, and different trips you want to save up for. Talk about your future. Talk about your money.

It's crazy to me that we will talk about our sex life to complete strangers, but you bring up the taboo subject of money, and it's like, "Whoa, I just said a bad word." It repels people. There are those money stories again that make us all clammy and embarrassed. But the more open conversations you have, the more comfortable and confident you will be together.

Mistake #5: Not Playing on the Same Team

Do you know how you can transfer money to a friend on Venmo? It could be for your share of half a pizza or how you pay someone back for snagging concert tickets. You can use it to send a quick $5 for a coffee for a friend (my personal favorite to receive and give, obviously), and it's currently one of the most convenient ways to transfer money instantly.

Another thing about Venmo is you can leave a note or an emoji to let the person you are sending or requesting money know what it's for. There's a public feed where you can see all your friends and their transactions. This last aspect seems like a strange concept, really, and a complete violation of privacy, but hey, what do I know?

Some of the comments get a little weird. One time, I noticed a friend had transferred money over to their spouse, and the memo said *"rent."* I was kinda confused because this friend had been married for over ten years, and they owned a house together. Then I saw another notice from another friend, another transfer to their spouse, only this one said *"groceries."* I started to pay closer attention to this feed. Do you know what I noticed? There were several transactions being made back and forth between married couples who were clearly splitting bills.

This is when it dawned on me: these couples have separate bank accounts. If they were sharing accounts, they wouldn't need to use Venmo to pay each other; they would simply transfer their money from their shared bank accounts and/or pay their mutual bills together. This also likely meant that they had divided up certain expenses and had their own bills they were personally paying, like in the case of rent. So not only were they not sharing bank accounts, but they also had their expenses divided up as if you were living with your roommate in college.

It didn't make sense to me. Why would you not join your money and work together to pay your bills? What were they afraid of? Did they not trust each other? Was this their idea of financial security if something were to happen and they were to split up? In most cases, it wouldn't matter if your accounts are separate (as we discussed above). In the case of divorce, your assets are split up anyway; it doesn't matter whose name is on the checking account. What does this say about your commitment to one another? Isn't it like having one foot in and the other out? I see no positive purpose or benefit to separating your money like this.

There is only one exception where I don't believe you should share money or accounts, and that's when your partner is intentionally or maybe even unintentionally harming you financially. Maybe they have a gambling addiction or are taking money out without talking with you. They might not currently have the self-discipline needed to get a grip on their spending, and this is putting you and them in imminent financial harm. They are lying to you, stealing, getting you deeper into debt, and the only way you can protect yourself is to maintain accounts they can't have access to. But this is a very different circumstance from simply not wanting to share bank accounts because you don't trust the other person enough to work together, or, more likely, because you don't want to give up control of "your" money.

When you get married, you become one. It's no longer mine and yours—it's ours. Everything in life you share—perhaps with the occasional "Don't touch my french fries I ordered" because "Joey doesn't share food!" Am I right? Sure, you don't need to share underwear or a toothbrush, but sharing the main resource that fuels your shared lives together and that's imperative.

One study found an enhanced quality in the relationship with couples who combine bank accounts. They felt more aligned with each other, and this also improved their confidence in handling money.[22] A 2022 study found that sharing bank accounts might even help marriages last longer: couples who pool all of their money (compared to couples who keep all or some of their money separate) experience greater relationship satisfaction and are less likely to break up.[23]

Ryan and I have shared bank accounts since the moment we were married. Not only did this set the tone for our marriage, but it also meant that not all the responsibility was placed on one person. It forced us to learn who the saver and the spender were. It made us more accountable for our spending since we weren't just living on a single income doing whatever we wanted. We had another person to consider. We ended up creating a pretty helpful system, which I now teach students in my program.

The foundation of our "Floodgate Financial Growth System" is creating five specific accounts to manage and sort your money. The five accounts are:

1. **Joint Account:** A basic account into which your paycheck is paid and from which all the bills are paid.
2. **Savings Account:** This account can be your emergency fund or security money.
3. **Giving Account:** Want to know the true secret to multiplying your money? I call it God magic, and it's when you faithfully give away money and allow the Holy Spirit to guide you to meet the needs and opportunities that arise. Do you want a Kingdom transformation in your bank account? Test God with your generosity and see what happens. When you have an account dedicated to giving, you get in the habit of testing God with your faithfulness. You get to meet the needs of others, and I must warn you, it becomes addicting!
4. **Fun Money Account:** This is to spend on literally anything you want together. Want to save up for a vacation? Nickname this account "Jamaica Money" and work together to reach your trip goals. Like to eat out a few times a week? Use this account to set aside money to indulge. There's one caveat to this account. The money must be *spent*. It's not a savings account; it's a spending account. Ramit Sethi says, "Spend extravagantly on the things you love and cut costs mercilessly on the things you don't." This is a great way to look at your priorities and discover what you actually want your money to be spent on. By having this account, you won't feel so limited by your budget, which in turn often leads to overspending or binging. Money is meant to be enjoyed, so use this account to enjoy it.
5. **Investing Account:** If you aren't getting your money to work for you, then you simply keep losing money to inflation and taxes and will never build wealth and security for your future. Use this account to invest in stocks, save up for a down payment on a rental, or to start

a business. The key here is not to let it sit there and tap into it when you get a flat tire. This is where you "pay yourself first" from each paycheck and make some money moves!

Next is one of the best tips I ever got from someone before we got married. I had asked this couple, "What's something you wish you would have done sooner in your marriage?" The advice was to have a "his and her" bank account separate from your joint account. That way, you don't have arguments around when he wants to buy a fishing boat and you just want to get your nails done. I thought it was amazing advice, and we implemented it that very next week. This single thing has prevented so many arguments and animosity that can build because, let's be honest, we have different wants and desires.

Here's how this works. In addition to the accounts listed above, you would open two checking accounts, one for each of you. We call this a *his* and *hers* checking account. In our budgeting, we have a monthly auto transfer into these two accounts. This is your own personal fun money, and how you spend it is entirely up to you. If you want to save up and buy a big-ticket item, go for it. Want to spend all the money each month? No problem. The point is to use these accounts for random spending that doesn't involve the other person. It's all *your* money.

What these accounts do is give you the independence and the freedom to spend guilt-free on yourself. Everything else is combined. This is the money that you use that doesn't include your partner. Ryan doesn't get his hair and nails done, and he doesn't value clothing as much as he values big-ticket items for his Jeep or outdoor gear. Now, instead of having arguments around money and nitpicking on who spent money on what or feeling guilty for buying something for yourself out of your joint money, you can't argue anything at all because you can spend that money in any way you want.

Having these separate accounts was one of the single best things we ever did to never argue about money again. Not only does this give you the independence you want, but it will also stop you both from harming your personal finances when you just feel like splurging. This helped us avoid going over budget, which often led to more stress paying the bills and more anger or blame toward each other.

I think a lot of issues when it comes to divorce over money can be solved by simply having more conversations around money early on. It's important to really be open and vulnerable with each other and have an understanding of your personal money stories and behaviors. You need to have raw, deep, meaningful, vulnerable conversations about your fears, your history, your spending, your goals, and what you want from life. If you do that before you get married, you're already going to set yourself up for way more success as you get into a relationship and into the commitment of marriage. And then, as you're in your marriage and you're having these meetings, you get to cheer each other on. You get to have different money conversations where you're no longer arguing, you're no longer frustrated, and you're no longer crying. You're no longer hiding the truth of how you feel. If you're having these conversations so often, it becomes like asking, "How was your day?" That's truly a transformational money and marriage experience.

CHAPTER 8

Your Kingdom Assignment

"The calling to follow Christ lies at the root of every other calling."[24]

You Are Called

You are uniquely qualified and gifted to specific assignments throughout your life that God has ordained, prepared, and destined just for you. We all have gifts and experiences God wants us to use to advance His Kingdom. The problem is that most people are drifting through life filled with fear, anxiety, and self-doubt, and many of us will never live the life God intended for us.

Most people know Napoleon Hill for *Think and Grow Rich*, an incredible book in which he outlined the "laws" of success after interviewing 25,000 ordinary people and 500 extraordinary outliers. It was a huge success. After that, Hill wrote *Outwitting the Devil*, which takes the form of an imaginary interview with the "root of all evil."

This book was so controversial that Hill never published it while he was alive. It was written in 1938 but wouldn't be published until 2011, 72 years later! When you read the book, you can get a sense that Hill was touching on some pretty controversial topics.

What was so unique about this book was the way that it was written. Hill wrote the book as if he was interviewing the devil. He asked questions about what kinds of tactics the devil uses to keep people from living their full potential. Hill illustrates how we spend our entire lives operating on the basis of either faith or fear.

In this fictitious interview with the devil, it's clear that the devil's goal is to make all humans aimless drifters who never get around to what we were meant to do in life. Throughout the book, Hill is trying to discover exactly how the "devil" is able to keep people drifting in life. A drifter is defined as "one who accepts whatever life throws in his way without making a protest or putting up a fight. He doesn't know what he wants from life and spends all of his time getting just that."

What's the opposite of someone who is drifting? Someone who is *driven*.

Those who are driven are different. The driven know they have something inside of them that is meant for more. They face obstacles and challenges just like the drifters, but they accept the challenges and move forward in faith and not fear.

Likely, if you're reading this book, you are driven. You feel a deep sense of purpose and that you were made for something special. You have these tugs, nudges, and gentle whispers that overcome your heart, and you just know God has something planned for you, but something is stopping you.

Refusing the Call

Joseph Campbell studied the most powerful myths from cultures around the world. He found that many of them follow a similar path. In his book *A Hero of a Thousand Faces*, he takes you through the "hero's" journey. Campbell said, "A hero is someone who has given his or her life to something bigger than oneself."

Every hero's journey starts with:

1. **The call to adventure.**
   This is where something or someone interrupts the hero's "ordinary life" to present a problem, threat, or opportunity.

2. **Refusal of the call.**

    The hero initially hesitates to embark on this journey and is unwilling to step out of their comfort zone or face their fear.

Can you remember a time when you felt the call to something bigger hit you, and you were like, *Whoa, this is it!* You are filled with such certainty, only to be met immediately with resistance, intimidation, and "impostor syndrome." You start to question everything. Fear creeps in, and you start talking yourself out of the very thing you feel called to do. This is the refusal of the call.

You aren't alone. Let's take a look at a few hero's journeys that you may or may not be familiar with and see how they refused the call.

In the movie *The Lion King*, Simba refuses the call.

In a tragic accident, his father is killed by his own brother, Scar. Simba thinks he is responsible for the death of his father, and Scar convinces Simba to run away and never return. So he leaves, letting the *shame and fear of rejection* stop him from his call to become king.

In the movie *Moana*, the title character feels this call to the ocean and knows she's meant to find answers for her island, but her father refuses to allow her to go past the reef. She lets *someone else's fear* stop her from her call to help her island.

In *The Lord of the Rings*, Frodo is hesitant to leave the Shire. He has no experience with the world outside. He lets his *lack of experience and the unknown* stop him from his call.

A hero refuses the journey because of fears and insecurities that have surfaced from the call to adventure. A hero is not willing to make the changes and prefers the safe haven of the ordinary world. Why is this?

Because it's so much easier to let fear take over instead of stepping out in faith, faith requires you to trust in the unknown. You do not have all the answers before you take the first step. Stepping into your calling requires something of yourself that isn't familiar. It requires you to accept a new identity you may not relate to.

I get it. You feel unqualified. You feel like you just don't know enough and aren't ready. You see so many other people doing what you want to do that you wonder, *Why should I even try? Someone's already doing it.* You're filled with so much doubt, and you feel like you're so unqualified.

But you know what?

"God doesn't call the qualified; He qualifies the called" (1 Corinthians 2:1-5).

And I've got news for you; your call is never small.

Abraham was given a "small calling" to leave the country, people, household, and everything he had ever known for a place he had never been to or heard of.

Noah's "small calling" was to build the ark that would survive the worldwide flood, fill it with two of every kind of animal, prepare enough food for them and his family to survive, and ride out a little storm. If the ark wasn't built correctly and had even the slightest gap for water to get in, all of humanity and animals left on Earth would have perished. No pressure! Noah's call was so big that scholars today still argue whether a boat this large and complex could have even been built. They estimate that it took 55 to 75 years to build.

Could you just imagine for a second how Noah would have felt about being tasked with something this big? What kind of doubts and fears would he have felt? Do you think he felt qualified or skilled enough to build this boat? Do you think he didn't have a single doubt in his mind that this calling was too big for him to carry out?

It was his faithfulness in God's plan that kept him going when he didn't know how, when, or what all of the details entailed.

What about Moses? His "small calling" was to lead the Israelites out of Egypt. *"Moses answered God, 'But why me? What makes you think that I could ever go to Pharaoh and lead the children of Israel out of Egypt?'" (Exodus 3:11-12).*

"I'll be with you," God said.

Every time Moses felt like he didn't have what it takes, that he didn't have the respect of the Israelites, or the knowledge, God went to great lengths to show that Moses was qualified. You can tell by this next verse just how much Moses lacked confidence, even in his voice.

"Master, please, I don't talk well. I've never been good with words, neither before nor after you spoke to me. I stutter and stammer" (Exodus 4:10).

I imagine this was one of Moses's biggest insecurities if he would actually plead with God not to send him because of it. Moses felt so embarrassed and unqualified simply because of a stutter.

God didn't care that he had a stutter. He called him to great things. I wonder how many of these excuses and seemingly insignificant details we all hold onto that keep us from answering the call with confidence and the faithfulness that will be required. I know I've always thought that I slur my words, talk too fast, and am not always articulate. Every few paragraphs or so as I type out this book, I wonder if the editors will think I failed grade school because of my poor spelling and grammar.

I'm not sure we're ever supposed to feel 100% qualified to do anything. In many ways, feeling like we're not fully capable humbles us, reminding us that we actually need God. It reinforces our dependency, not on ourselves, but on Him.

God Qualifies the Called, and Your Call Is Never Small

Here's what we can learn from the call to adventure.

1. Answer the call.
- Even if it doesn't make sense
- Even if others don't understand it
- Even if it seems impossible
- Even if we're afraid
- Even if you don't feel worthy
- Even if you don't feel qualified

These are not requirements to follow the call.

2. **Your calling will bless others.**

Someone needs what's on the other side of your calling. Prosperity, success, abundance, and living a purposeful life aren't about you. It's about the needs that will be met on the other side of that call. God doesn't say, "You're blessed to live a blessed and full life for thyself." He says you're blessed to be a blessing *("I will bless you; I will make your name great, and you will be a blessing." [Genesis 12:2]).* For you to be a blessing, you must first be blessed.

"The blessing of the Lord brings wealth without painful toil for it" (Proverbs 10:22).

The blessing of the Lord brings something with it. It brings something into your life. You don't have to pursue the blessing. Blessings simply require you to obey. Money is never *the* blessing; it's the byproduct of God's open doors, wisdom, and favor.

"If you fully obey the Lord your God and you carefully follow all his commands, the Lord your God will set you on high above all nations on earth, and all these blessings will come upon you and accompany you if you obey the Lord your God" (Deuteronomy 28:1-3)

Could you imagine if Moses hadn't answered the call? If he had let his fear, his doubts, and his feelings of being unqualified stop him? He couldn't have led his people to safety, to the land God had promised them. The call was for them, the entire nation of Israel, and their future, not for him. He never got to set foot in the promised land.

God will shape our character and identity through our call. But often, we are so busy judging ourselves and thinking we are selfish in our desire to answer the call that we lose sight of how God might want to use us and our gifts for His glory and purpose.

In a conversation with one of my dearest friends, we got to talking about her business. She owns an incredible event business and is one of the most talented people I know, but she was struggling with feeling irresponsible for the business she has created. She felt that what she creates and produces in her business creates waste and hurts the planet. She was struggling with how there is not enough water in the world and how deforestation is impacting our planet. She was worried about the population of the world being too big and somehow connected her business to all these major problems in the world. This left her feeling the weight of the world on her shoulders. And while these are causes to be concerned and conscious about, they had absolutely nothing to do with her business.

She was viewing the world from a poverty mindset, much like the finite slice of pie I mentioned in the previous chapter. She felt that her contributions—using the skills, abilities, and talents God gave her—were taking more from the world than they were giving. This was the exact opposite of what her business did. Her skills are a blessing to every single client she works with, and she creates spaces for people to connect in the most beautiful ways.

She struggled with the fact that, while there were people suffering and major problems in the world, her business was prospering. It didn't feel fair. This is something she termed the "fairness fetish." It's beautiful, really, because you see so much compassion in her worry. But truly, her success in her business has nothing to do with people not having access to clean water.

So I played a little devil's advocate and asked her, "What do you think the solution is? Do you think you should close your business and not continue serving people with your skills? Then, after you shut your doors, you just move into a log cabin in the woods, off the grid somewhere without electricity, plant a garden, collect rainwater, and live off the land? All because you are worried you are leaving a carbon footprint on the world?"

What does that do for anyone? Isn't that a little selfish when you think about it? So you aren't releasing as much carbon emissions or whatever limits she had in her mind, but who is she serving then? Who is she able to bless? How is she helping to solve the very issues she's so worried about? How is that going to provide clean water wells or help people out of poverty?

The truth is that we can't serve the hungry, orphans, and widows if we are poor; we simply become part of the bigger problem. Only when we fix our circumstances and finances can we truly become part of the solution. How much more could you bless others when you come from a place of strength and not weakness? I don't think we should be so overly concerned with all the details of how we are serving with what God has blessed us with.

It seemed to me that my friend wanted to make a different impact outside of her current business. However, the way I see it is that her business could serve not only in the marketplace but also as the vehicle to help serve in the mission.

I think a better question to ask yourself is, *If not me, who?*

You see, God's plan will happen with or without you. As Matthew 6:10 puts it, *"Thy kingdom come. Thy will be done on earth, as it is in heaven."*

Whether you ignore the call or not, God has a plan. And if not you, He will call upon someone else. I don't know about you, but that motivates me. Knowing that God has placed something on my heart that He has uniquely qualified me to pursue, then watching someone else live it out, drives me to want to step out in faith more. Have you ever felt that? You see someone doing the same thing you want to do, saying the same things you say, and walking on a path you see for yourself. There is a sense of jealousy watching that happen—we are human. Instead of envying what someone else is doing or comparing yourself (which is pointless), use that jealousy to fuel you and motivate you. That jealousy is an internal signal of something you desire. There is some truth to that jealousy, so explore that more to get clarity on *why you* can also do the dang thing!

Notice I didn't say *how*. Tony Robbins says, "Avoid the tyranny of how. Immersion is how you learn." Often, we get so paralyzed by all the details of how we are going to do something. We create our beautiful to-do list, break down our bubble graphs into actionable steps, take those steps, and put them in our perfectly color-coordinated calendar. These are all great ways to break down your goals, but the key step to transformation in your life is to take action. You have to immerse yourself in the thing you want to do to become an expert and learn.

> *You don't learn by creating the plan; you learn by putting the plan into action.*

The tyranny of how keeps you stuck in the unknown, stuck in analysis paralysis, stuck because you don't want to make the wrong decision. It stops you dead in your tracks from fulfilling the call.

Think about Noah and the ark. I'm sure he had a lot of "How in the heck am I going to do this?" moments. How is he going to get all the animals on board? How is he going to design the boat to withstand the storm? How is he going to convince his family to join him, etc.? You're not going to know how. God's call hardly ever includes a step-by-step manual with a detailed timeline. God's call requires faith, not facts. God often tells us what to do before He shows us how to do it.

Truly successful people have learned to persevere and not let the question of "How?" stop them from achieving their goals.

Let's use Elon Musk as an example. Elon Musk is the CEO of SpaceX and Tesla. He's disrupted multiple industries. When he started SpaceX, he had no background in aerospace, but he was determined to reduce space travel costs. He had a clear vision and wanted to push the limits to impact the costs of aerospace and how this would impact the future. Similarly, with Tesla, he entered the automotive industry with no prior experience, but he wanted to succeed in revolutionizing electric cars. He embarked on this journey without full knowledge or certainty of success. I highly recommend you watch his documentary, *The Real Life Iron Man*, where you can see how much he is driven by passion, perseverance, and willingness to learn and adapt along the way.

His story illustrates that achieving the impossible often involves stepping into the unknown, taking risks, and being persistent despite initial limitations. Elon Musk was one rocket launch away from total failure. One more rocket.

If one more rocket exploded, he was done. But it was the perseverance of one more rocket that allowed him to break through this industry in massive ways. He didn't know how. He answered the call. Think about all of the refusals of the call. In this documentary, he talks about how passionate he was about aerospace and the space industry and how it had inspired him as a kid. He talks about how every single person he ever looked up to thought he was stupid and unqualified. It was heartbreaking to him because all he cared about was solving a problem. He knew he had skills, talents, and determination, but he didn't know how. He pursued it anyway.

Your Calling Takes Time

When Saul was traveling to Damascus and had a come-to-Jesus moment, it wasn't until after another ten years of his faithfulness and spiritual growth that he would get his assignment. Moses was 80 years old when he confronted the pharaoh and led the Israelites out of Egypt.

Take a look at some more modern-day examples. Juliette Gordon Low founded the Girl Scouts of America when she was 51 years old. Julia Child published her first cookbook when she was 49. *Mastering the Art of French Cooking* became a bestseller and led to her becoming a renowned chef and television personality. Vera Wang transitioned from a figure skater and fashion editor to a fashion designer, launching her own highly acclaimed bridal gown collection. She was 40. Colonel Harland Sanders founded Kentucky Fried Chicken (KFC) when he was 65. Maya Angelou published her autobiography, *I Know Why the Caged Bird Sings*, when she was 41. It became a critically acclaimed bestseller, launching her career as a prolific writer, poet, and civil rights activist.

Your Kingdom assignment takes time. Most of us aren't willing to wait. We're not willing to be patient. We're not willing to let our experiences shape us. The truth is that God doesn't need us. Maybe you don't want to hear that. The Creator of the universe and everything in it does not need us, but He desires a relationship with us, and He wants to shape our character to be more like Him. And He does that time and time again with people in the Bible. He does that by presenting experiences and opportunities that shape our character. Every single calling takes time. Why wouldn't that be the same for you?

In a sermon I once heard, the pastor said, "What seems pointless is often preparation." This hit me hard. I don't know about you, but I often ask God, "When will it be my time?" or "When will this door open?" The pastor was talking about Joseph and his entire lifelong journey. Joseph was known to his siblings as his father's favorite child, and this upset his brothers, so one day, his brothers turned on him and sold him into slavery. He would eventually spend two years in prison, where God gave him the gift of interpreting dreams. One of the prisoners for whom Joseph interpreted a dream would go on to work for the pharaoh of Egypt. A few years later, the pharaoh needed help interpreting dreams. This servant remembered Joseph, and the pharaoh sent for him to interpret his dreams. Joseph's gift of interpreting dreams would lead him to serve the pharaoh and manage and prepare food for the seven years of famine.

Joseph would have a full circle moment with his brothers and find healing and redemption through his experience. I am sure that Joseph questioned the point of it all along that journey. Don't you think Joseph had every right to feel like his life was wasting away, not understanding why he was wrongly imprisoned, that he at times felt like everything was pointless? Look how God shaped him through every experience.

Even your smallest assignment can lead to your biggest breakthroughs!

Here's the last point I want to drive home.

Absolutely Nothing Can Thwart God's Plans

"Now to him who is able to do far more abundantly than all that we ask or think, according to the power at work within us" (Ephesians 3:20).

God is working despite all things and above all things. His plan never fails. God is committed to the plan. The question is, "Are you?"

It's time to stop comparing our calling to that of anyone else. Do you know what makes your path different? You. You're the differentiator. There's only one you, and that makes what you are called to do unique. Many of us will have similar callings, but there's only one of you.

The only difference between where you are and the people you admire is that they were driven. They still faced all the same challenges. They had a point where they refused the call. They faced their fear, and they continued to push through in faith. The enemy wants nothing more than for you to be filled with distractions, doubts, and feelings of being sucked dry of time and resources so that you never fulfill God's call.

Your faithfulness to your Kingdom assignment is going to be rewarded. Some of the last words of Jesus recorded in scripture were, *"Behold, I am coming soon! My reward is with me, and I will give to every one according to what he has done"* (Revelation 22:12).

God will reward you. This is on top of the reward of eternal life. We are saved by faith alone, not by works, but we will be rewarded by our good works of that faith. God's going to reward you for the sacrifices that you've made and the work that you have done. It matters to Him. Your assignment doesn't have an ending. It doesn't end when you've reached a milestone or accomplished a big life goal. It doesn't end when you have secured financial freedom for your family or paid off your debt. It doesn't involve a cabin in the woods where you hide off the grid waiting for Jesus to return. The entire idea of retirement in the modern-day context is not biblical.

How will you know when your Kingdom assignment is complete? When He calls you home. As long as you are still breathing, you are not done. And if you're committed to the plan, if you're committed to the call like God is committed, how different would your life look?

God is purposeful. He's not going to give you a call that you cannot complete. He's not going to put plans into action that He doesn't follow through on.

I have a tattoo on my wrist that says, "I am an arrow in my Father's hands." It reminds me that God's got me in His hands and that He has released me into this world with purpose. I have been redeemed and refined for His glory. He's pulled back the branch and filed the shaft straight. He's chiseled the tip of the arrow and fashioned the fletching just right for the arrow to fly. He has released me into this world to hit my target. To find and love Him, to love and bless others, and to follow faithfully where God has asked me to go.

It's time to go all in! You were uniquely created and qualified by God for a full and abundant life in all areas. It is through sin that there is suffering and hardship, but this wasn't the original plan God had in store. Your calling will push you and shape you in ways that bring you closer to Him. What are you waiting for?

Exercise:

If you are still struggling with knowing the path you are supposed to follow, take some time to answer these questions. By finding the answers and making the decision, we can start to use fear as our compass and walk by faith, pursuing our path with confidence, trust, and without limits.

Who is God calling you to become?

_____

_____

_____

_____

Who is he calling you to serve?

And what opportunities has he given you right now?

CHAPTER 9

Becoming a Trailblazer

"You must do the thing you think you cannot do."
–Eleanor Roosevelt

It was just like any other day. I had recently returned to my retail manager job after a torturous eight months of purchasing a wedding venue, building a 40-by-80-foot two-story barn, and hosting my first summer full of weddings, all to have it ripped from my hands and be stripped of any belief that I could run and operate a successful business of my own. I had lost over half a million dollars and was doing everything I could to avoid bankruptcy in the process. I was devastated. We had gotten involved with the wrong people. They eagerly took advantage of us, knowing we would be facing a very long lawsuit with the chance that we would never recover anything financially. Ten years later, I can confirm we never did.

I was in so much heartache and pain that I would burst out in tears throughout the day for weeks and months to follow. I would replay everything in my head over and over again like a broken record, reliving the pain and abuse I experienced every single day. It was the second hardest grief I had felt outside of losing my father when I was 20 years old. I felt hopeless and like a complete and utter failure. So I went back to work doing the only thing I knew I was good at—retail. With my tail tucked between my legs, I asked for my old job as a manager back. I thought it would just be temporary, but now, here I was a year later and still helping style women in a new pair of denim as I tended to my wounds. I was great at retail sales, one of the best in the industry. It's what I knew and I had more than 20 years of experience. I could sell clothing with my eyes closed and not in the sleazy car salesman way. I understood people and the ways they shopped. I knew how to dress their body types and personalities and how to build customers for life. It was on the sales floor that I was most confident—where I knew I couldn't screw up. Who was I to think I could switch career paths? I tried and failed miserably, so clearly, I should just go back to what I knew.

I had just closed up the store and headed to go work out. Beside me were the same incredible women I would see daily as we would sweat and shake together in our daily Pure Barre class. We all had our favorite spots to set up at the bar, and we had become so accustomed to the workout that we could probably do it in our sleep. Towards the end of the workout, we would do our quick ab set before stretching. On this day, the instructor said something that would forever change my life. While we were tucking away and working our abs, she asked, "Are you in your comfort zone, or are you in your war zone? The change you want happens in your war zone."

Now, obviously, she was talking about the workout and encouraging us to push a little harder for these last few minutes, but at that moment, all I could think about was where I was in my life. Here I was back at my retail manager job, which I had now done for several companies over the last two decades. I was clocking in, closing up, helping customers, working out, going home to my dogs, and falling asleep watching another episode of *Friends* before waking up to do it all over again. I was living the same routine life I was familiar with, one that felt safe and consistent. I was in my comfort zone. I liked being there because then I knew what to expect. It was predictable, and knowing what needed to be done at my job left me feeling secure and confident. The last time I tried something new, it didn't work out, so I wanted to just stay in my comfort zone where I couldn't get hurt.

As I was on my mat and pushing myself to crunch a little harder, I realized that I was so afraid of failing that I had accepted I was never going to try anything out of my comfort zone again. Tears started dripping down my face as I realized how change, growth, healing, and fulfillment weren't going to happen if I stayed here. Was I in my comfort zone? Absolutely. Was I happy? Not at all. If I wanted to change my life and my circumstances, I needed to be brave enough to step into the war zone. The next day, when I went to work, I submitted my notice without knowing where I was headed, but I desperately wanted a change in my life. Change is hard and scary, but like the instructor said, "Change only happens in the war zone." Comfort zones are confusing, too, because they are places where you might be experiencing wins or places where you are likely very competent.

In his book *The Big Leap*, Gay Hendricks outlines four distinct zones people operate in, each with varying levels of fulfillment and effectiveness.

1. **Zone of Incompetence**
    This zone consists of tasks or skills that individuals are not proficient in and should delegate or avoid altogether to focus on their strengths.
2. **Zone of Competence**
    Here, individuals perform tasks they are competent in but don't necessarily excel at. While these tasks may be necessary, they shouldn't be the focus of one's time and energy.
3. **Zone of Excellence**
    This zone encompasses tasks individuals excel at and receive recognition and praise for. However, despite the competence and success achieved here, it may not fully tap into their true potential.
    This was what was confusing for me when it came to retail management. I enjoyed it for the most part. I had ranked at the top in sales for every company I have worked for, and I truly loved building relationships with my clients. It was my comfort zone and also my zone of excellence, but it wasn't where I felt the most

fulfilled. I was always left feeling like there was something more for me.

4. **Zone of Genius**

    This is the ultimate zone where individuals operate in their unique talents and strengths, experiencing maximum fulfillment and effectiveness. In this zone, one's work feels effortless and aligns deeply with one's passion and purpose, leading to exceptional results and personal satisfaction.

My question to you is, "What zone are you in? Are you in your comfort zone or war zone?" Maybe, like me, you feel called, assigned, and meant for something more, but you're unconsciously living in your comfort zone because of fear of failure, fear of success, and fear of the unknown.

I saw an interview with Will Smith in which he spoke about how failure is part of the process of success. He said, "Fail fast. Fail often. Fail forward." I felt a sense of relief, as if fear didn't have a grip on me anymore. If failure was part of the process to success, then it was a guarantee I would have to face it. I know this now and have experienced lots of different failures along my journey, but the difference now is that I don't wrap my identity around failure. *I* am not a failure; failure is simply a part of the process. Fear is necessary. It keeps us alive and stops us from jumping in front of a moving vehicle, but it doesn't need to be in the driver's seat.

I knew I had to start operating in my war zone because I believed God was calling me to do something more. I was going to be uncomfortable, and walking into the next phase of life was going to feel unfamiliar. It was going to require me to find a new identity and step out of all the lies I was telling myself.

How does this pertain to your financial life? We all know we need to spend less, save more, and invest in our future. Why don't we do it? Why isn't it that simple? The problem is that it feels out of character. Your current identity might be that you think you aren't good with money. If you identify as someone who isn't good with money, it's *impossible* for you to also identify as someone who is great with money. You are either one or the other, and whichever one you believe will have the greatest impact on your reality. There is a saying that your thoughts become your words, your words become your actions, your actions become your habits, your habits become your character, and your character becomes your destiny.

When something feels out of character, it feels uncomfortable. If you believe you are not good with money, your behaviors will likely match that. You will avoid it. You will ignore your spending. You will likely overspend and live above your means. You would rather stick your head in the sand than deal with the fact that you don't know how you are going to pay your credit card bill at the end of the month because this is the character and behavior of someone who believes they aren't good with money. Maybe you want to blame your current circumstances, your job, your spouse, the economic conditions, or the bank. You want to blame your parents and how they didn't teach you, or the lack of financial education in the church or our schools. We will come up with all sorts of reasons to justify our current identity.

My identity was "I'm not good at business. I'm a failure. I am only good at being an employee." If I had never changed this identity, I would still be comfortably working as a manager, believing I was never good enough to have my own successful business. I wanted to blame the people I was involved with, and certainly, there was foul play on their part. But was I going to continue crying over my morning toast, blaming them for my struggles forever? Was I going to add "victim" to the badges of honor I wore effortlessly on my arm, or was I going to come out of the wilderness more refined and renewed?

If I wanted to change my life, behaviors, and outcomes, I had to change my identity. Changing your identity requires you to believe things about yourself and your character even when your circumstances don't match. For example, I can say, "I am going to be a millionaire!" but it's really hard to relate and feel like a millionaire when you're not sure if you can afford groceries that week. Changing your identity is one of the hardest things to fix. It requires us to change not only our actions but also our self-perception, which is more difficult because we have lived with these behaviors and beliefs for so long.

Paving the Way

On May 6, 1954, a 25-year-old medical student named Roger Bannister became the first recorded human to shatter the elusive barrier of the four-minute mile, completing the mile run in an astonishing 3 minutes and 59.4 seconds. Before this, the world record for a mile was 4 minutes and 1.3 seconds, which was set by Gunder Hägg in 1945. The four-minute mile barrier stood for decades. Prior to Bannister's momentous milestone, runners had been actively chasing this goal since 1886, involving the collaboration of some of the best coaches and most gifted athletes across the globe.

British journalist John Bryant, who wrote the book *3:59.4: The Quest to Break the 4-Minute Mile*, states, "For years milers had been striving against the clock, but the elusive four minutes had always beaten them. It had become as much a psychological barrier as a physical one. And like an unconquerable mountain, the closer it was approached, the more daunting it seemed."[25]

But just 46 days after Bannister's feat, another athlete named John Landy would break the barrier again, with a time of 3 minutes and 58 seconds. One year later, three runners would break this four-minute barrier *in a single race*. Today, the "four-minute barrier" has been broken by over 1,700 athletes and is now considered a relatively standard performance for professional middle-distance runners.

So what shifted? Experts have studied this momentous milestone and emphasize it as more of a mental achievement than a physical one. When Roger Bannister accomplished this lofty goal, people realized that it was possible for them to do so, too. He was the trailblazer.

A trailblazer is a pioneer, someone who's willing to take risks and go on a path that isn't already there. They blaze a trail, and they leave a path for others.

These runners now knew what was possible because someone had achieved the "impossible." They had a real example, which gave them the belief that they could do it, too. Right now, you might not have any examples of people close to you who have accomplished the level of success, achievement, and financial freedom that you desire for yourself. Many of us don't. I didn't come from money. I didn't personally know any millionaires or successful business owners. There's something significant about seeing someone else pave the way and show you a path that helps you understand what's possible. You see that if they can do it, you can do it too. You know how I mentioned that your calling blesses other people? There's someone else on the other side of your calling that needs you to become the trailblazer. People desperately need what you have, and you are underserving them by hiding.

There is someone in your life who needs you to be the trailblazer—whether it be your children, your spouse, your siblings, your friends, or some stranger who's watching on the internet. They need to see someone breaking chains and barriers.

If you are reading this book, I have no doubt *you* are the trailblazer.

Yes, *you*!

You're the one who's going to pave the way for generations to come. No one else is going to do it. No one else cares enough. To become a trailblazer, you are going to have to blaze your own trail. It won't be easy, and like any real adventure, it's going to require grit, determination, the ability to withstand some rough weather, and a desire so big it propels you toward your summit.

What is the legacy you want to leave? I always hear people say they want to pass on generational wealth. What does that mean? As we noted above, 70% of generational wealth doesn't make it past the second generation, and 90% disappears by the third.

> ***Your money and your wealth don't transfer.***
> ***Your knowledge will.***

Money will come, and it will go. It will be there, and it won't. But money skills, education, and financial literacy last generations. And that's going to require you to become the trailblazer in your family by leading the way. It's going to require you to get uncomfortable. It's going to require you to write a new story. It's going to require you to find and shape a new identity.

Think about the traits and stories of some of the most successful people. Hardworking, passionate, driven, resilient. They believe they can even when everybody else is telling them otherwise. They try, fail, and get back up and try again. Trailblazers embrace the journey, knowing there will be difficult times on the trail.

I've done some tough hikes before. I recently climbed Mt. Kilimanjaro and have been hiking and playing in the dirt from a very young age. But let me tell you the hardest trail I've ever hiked that you've probably never heard of. I love to adventure outdoors and explore new places. There's something so beautiful about being in nature and pushing your physical limits in pursuit of the views.

Two years after I left my retail job and decided to fully embrace my war zone, my husband and I, along with a good friend, decided we wanted to climb the highest peak in Montana, Granite Peak. Up to this point, I had been on countless hikes and excursions, but I'd never climbed a mountain this big. We had spent the whole summer hiking, camping, and fishing and didn't think much about the difficulty of this summit. We had talked with some locals and friends who had hiked the peak before and decided to take the more challenging but scenic route. Our plan was to hike eight miles to Princess Lake, a remote lake away from the busier trail, and camp the night so we could get an early start the next morning to the summit. We woke up, heated some dehydrated egg scramble summit food, and headed up the trail by 7:00 a.m.

The next five hours were some of the most beautiful hiking I have ever experienced. We followed the creek through the valley, where we passed four small lakes of the Snowball Lakes chain. There was a lot of boulder hopping, and we were thankful that the cairns were well-placed on this route, making it easy to stay on the trail. Once past these lakes, we were met with fields of wildflowers and our first view of Avalanche Lake. It was breathtaking. After hiking approximately 10 miles, we finally arrived at the scenic and inspiring Avalanche Lake, which rested at the foot of Granite Peak. We stopped for a quick break to eat and fill up our water. We could hear the echo in the valley as the first few climbers shouted from the top of the peak in celebration of their summit. It was just the energy boost we needed to start what would be the most difficult part of the trip so far. We were excited and ready to push through.

Our excitement quickly turned into frustration as we started climbing up a seemingly endless expanse of granite scree, which is simply broken rock fragments up a very steep portion of the climb. This was one of the most dangerous portions of the climb because you are faced with rockfall that can and has swept hikers away. Hiking up on this scree was excruciating. For every step you took forward, your next step would set you two steps back. It was a constant battle to find good footing and prevent a rockslide from sweeping you to the base. We were exposed to the ruthless sun at its peak in the sky and spent much of our time getting up this mile-and-a-half portion of the mountain using both our hands and feet.

By the time we got to the saddle, we were exhausted, out of water, and it was now very late in the afternoon. At this point, we could see hikers still heading toward the summit, so we decided to push through and speed up, given that we were running out of daylight. The sky was clear, but we knew that by pushing forward, we would be guaranteed to have to hike back to

Princess Lake in the dark. We were naively willing to take this risk to reach the summit.

As we started the approach, it felt good to finally be on solid ground—until we reached the snow bridge, that is. This was a snow-packed section of the path that we had to cross, knowing one foot on either side of you would be certain death if you slipped or the snow gave out under you. Our time and daylight were running out fast, so we forewent the extra rope safety and steadily crossed the snow-packed trail, placing one foot firmly in front of the other. My heart was pounding. One wrong step and this trip was going to turn from bad to worse.

Once we got across safely, we noticed a few trekkers ahead of us turning back. They were so close to the summit but probably did the right thing by turning back. We, on the other hand, felt like we had come too far to give up now. This kind of stubbornness can get you hurt in conditions like these, and if I'm being honest, we made a lot of bad decisions on this trip and put ourselves in unnecessary danger.

As the last two trekkers started to make their way back, we were now the only three people left on the mountain, and we had less than an hour of sunlight left. My only goal was to get to the top and back to the saddle before it was pitch black. There was no way I was going to cross the snow bridge at night. So we pushed forward. Again, we skipped the extra rope safety, as we were all pretty good climbers and needed to get up as quickly as we could. Each hand and foot was meticulously placed as we worked our way up.

Around the time we made it to the saddle, Ryan started complaining about feeling sick. Apparently, he had saved some of the egg scramble from that morning and finished it off for lunch. By that point, this food had been in his warm backpack for over 5 hours. I had no idea that was what we had eaten for lunch, and now he was dehydrated, sick, and becoming weaker by the hour. My friend and I watched over him as he led us up the final finger of the ascent. Once at the top, we were completely overjoyed. Tears streamed down my face as we hugged each other and took in the views. We shouted from the bottom of our lungs because we had accomplished such a huge accomplishment. Only 50% of people attempting Granite Peak make it to the summit, and here we were with 360-degree views of the largest mountain range in Montana. I will never forget the rush, relief, and sense of accomplishment I felt. We stayed there for less than 10 minutes, though, because we were now facing the most dangerous part, the descent. Did you know about 75% of falls during mountain hiking occur during descent?[26]

Going up a steep portion of the peak was way easier than going down. This time, we had to get the ropes out so we could safely rappel down a few sections. I watched, horrified, as my weak, sick husband headed down the rope first. All three of us were now hyperaware of his declining condition and extra vigilant on our safety checks with our harnesses. The sun had set, and the clouds had rolled in. It was getting darker and grayer by the minute. Little did we know the thrill and excitement of our accomplishment would be a fading memory as our trip took a dramatic turn for the worse. I had one goal: to get to the saddle before it was pitch black, but every few minutes, Ryan had to stop as he got sick yet again. By the time we finally arrived back at the saddle, we had all been without water for over five hours as we watched the last bit of light in the sky fade to darkness.

We still had another 11 miles back to our camp and another eight miles back to the car from there. We were in a race against time because our friend had told her mom that if she did not hear back from us by 9:00 p.m. (exactly 24 hours from now), she should call for help. At this point, with no water for over six hours, Ryan was cold, weak, and moving at a snail's pace. It took every bit of energy for him to put one foot in front of the other. I knew I was going to have to lead us back to camp, so I took Ryan's backpack along with my own, and we faced the scree field in pitch-black conditions. There wasn't a sliver of moonlight in the sky. Every 50 steps or so, we would all turn off our headlamps, and I would give my eyes a few seconds to adjust to the dark—it was the only way I could see if we were heading in the right direction. After a few minutes, I could just make out a faint, dark glimmer of Avalanche Lake.

That was my marker. Ryan was a zombie and fell multiple times on the scree. It was pure luck—and maybe some of God's protection—that he didn't break a leg or have some of the moving boulders pin him down. I tried to direct every step for him by taking the first one, but that mile-and-a-half scree scramble was a test of strength for us all.

By the time we arrived at the lake, it was now just past midnight. It had taken 12 hours for us to make it back to our lunch spot. I rushed to pump us each several liters of filtered water, and we chugged it down. I've never wanted water so badly in my life, and it was exactly what Ryan needed to regain some energy. Once you stop moving, though, your sweat starts to cool, and with the cold glacial water we were drinking, we started to get cold in the high altitude. We had to keep moving because the last thing we needed was to become hypothermic.

We filled up our water and started the 10-mile trek back to camp. The sound of the creek was now guiding me, as I had no trail or marker in sight. As we passed the lake, we had a new challenge present itself. Less than 20 yards in front of us, we could see several sets of glowing eyes reflecting off our headlamps. The scent of our bodies and curiosity led a herd of mountain goats right in our way. There were easily eight to 10 goats, and while we tried to scare them off with loud noises and big bodily gestures to get them to scatter, they held their ground. We now had to make our way safely around them, which led us to a cliffside we couldn't get down. We had to head back to where we met them and get through without being charged. We knew the goats were on the trail we needed to follow to get back to the Snowball Lakes. We grabbed some big rocks and threw them in the direction of the goats to try and startle them and break up the herd. With our sticks in our hands, we linked arms to appear bigger, and we went for it. We yelled, they scattered, and we finally made it past them. Once past them, we found a giant cairn (a human-made pile or stack of stones) and knew we were heading in the right direction.

From here until Princess Lake, there wasn't a trail. It was a boulder field across the creek, and an hour in, I got disoriented. We were so tired, running on no calories since we had run out of snacks hours ago, and I was starting to shiver uncontrollably. We pulled out our map and compass and tried to get our bearings again. This was a breaking point for me. I had been powering through on adrenaline and fear and had been pushing through all the hurdles along the way, but I hit my wall. Ryan was feeling better and took the lead to get us back to our camp. We hadn't said a word to each other in hours.

When we finally arrived at the edge of Princess Lake, the sunrise started to peek through, and I fell to my knees and released a huge cry. On the one hand, I was relieved because we made it back to the tent. On the other hand, I knew we still had to pack up our gear and still had another eight relentless miles back to the car. I felt completely broken on the inside. I had decided at that moment that I wanted to leave my backpack and all my gear on that mountain. There wasn't a single ounce of me that wanted to ever hike again, so I wouldn't need it anyway.

Of course, I was desperate, still dehydrated, and completely malnourished by this point. We had just hiked for 24 hours straight on less than 2,000 calories each. We were so exhausted, but we had to try and sleep, so we crashed in the tent, woke up a few hours later, packed up all our gear, and set out for the trailhead.

The next eight hours were the quietest hike I have ever been on with two other people. Not a single word. We were all in a deep, dark place, trying to find our inner motivation to keep persevering. Our packs were heavier with our gear, and our feet were screaming. I don't remember much about that last eight miles, but I do remember the last view I took in of the valley I would hope to never see again—I was never coming back. We made it back to our car and raced to get into cell phone reception. It was 10:00 p.m., and our friend's mom was about to call search and rescue when she finally heard from us. We were alive.

That mountain took something from me that day, but it wouldn't be until several months later that I would be able to recognize what I had gained. It was the hardest physical and mental challenge I had ever put myself through.

The unexpected gain from this experience was knowing I could do something I didn't think I was capable of. As I started facing business challenges or would come up on a difficult real estate project where things weren't quite going my way, I found myself thinking, *If I can survive Granite Peak, I can do anything.* Granite Peak had now become the bar of how much I could endure, how much resilience I had, and the strength I didn't know I had inside. I think that's why athletes push themselves beyond their physical capabilities: they realize how much strength is needed in their minds and just how capable they are.

What's your Granite Peak?

Have you ever experienced this kind of challenge that has now become a standard, or are you in your comfort zone, playing it safe with no real understanding of what you can accomplish? I've found a love for pushing myself physically because of what that does for me mentally and how that gets applied in my everyday life. It helps me realize that I can do hard things.

I want you to visualize something with me for a few minutes. I want you to think about a huge, scary goal you have in life. Do you want to write a book? Be a public speaker? Do you want to build a multimillion-dollar business? Do you want to compete in the Olympics? What is this big audacious goal you have in life?

My big, scary goal is:

_____

_____

_____

_____

This is your Granite Peak.

Now, imagine you are standing at the trailhead, excited and ready to start your adventure toward the summit. All you have with you is a map, compass, and a backpack. You hit the trail with excitement and a little bit of "What the heck am I doing?" energy. A few miles into your hike, you come to a dense forest, and there's no clear sight of a trail. Do you turn back and follow the trail back to your car? Or do you press forward? You have no idea what is in this forest or what dangers lie ahead, but your determination to reach the summit pushes you to keep going. You pull out your map and compass to get a sense of direction. Your mind is telling you to turn back. Who are you to think you can climb this summit? What are you even doing here? You aren't qualified! It feels scary and impossible, but that fear is your compass, and it's pointing right into the forest.

I think a lot of you reading this are in this place. You are stuck in shame, guilt, and "impostor syndrome," feel unworthy, and are paralyzed by fear. You've taken a few steps, but you can't see what's past the forest or roadblocks in your way. Because you can't see the summit in front of you, you don't know if this is the "right way." I know you don't want to turn back, but it feels impossible to move forward. If there's one lesson I learned on my summit, it was that the only certain choice I had to make was to keep moving forward. The only way I was going to get up or down that mountain was with one step at a time, even when I couldn't see the trail in pitch black. Even when I didn't think I had the energy to go on. Even when I thought it would never end.

Trailblazers create a new path before them. One that isn't there. Every trail, every summit, every human barrier had a trailblazer. Someone willing to push through the fear and blaze the trail for themselves and for others to follow.

Trailblazers reach for new heights. Trailblazers shatter ceilings. Trailblazers defy societal norms. Trailblazers seize opportunities. Trailblazers aren't afraid of financial gain. Trailblazers understand that money is a tool and that they can use it for good. Trailblazers are innovative. Trailblazers want to pave the way for others.

That voice, the one in the background that says, *Really? You? What qualifications do you have?* That's your old identity, your old money story, the "Poverty Mind" speaking nonsense at you so that you feel insecure and incapable.

Let's take a look at the journey of one incredible trailblazer, a woman who paved the way for us and showed us what's possible.

Proverbs 31 Woman

You have likely heard of the Proverbs 31 Woman. Much of the time we consider her as a virtuous, kind, wonderful mother, family woman, and nice business owner, but as you dive into her story, she's nothing short of an incredible trailblazer.

The Woman Who Fears the Lord

"An excellent wife who can find?
She is far more precious than jewels.
The heart of her husband trusts in her,
and he will have no lack of gain.
She does him good and not harm,
all the days of her life.
She seeks wool and flax,
and works with willing hands.
She is like the ships of the merchant;
she brings her food from afar.
She rises while it is yet night
and provides food for her household
and portions for her maidens.
She considers a field and buys it;
with the fruit of her hands, she plants a vineyard.

*She dresses herself with strength
and makes her arms strong.
She perceives that her merchandise is profitable.
Her lamp does not go out at night.
She puts her hands to the distaff,
and her hands hold the spindle.
She opens her hand to the poor
and reaches out her hands to the needy.
She is not afraid of snow for her household,
for all her household is clothed in scarlet.
She makes bed coverings for herself;
her clothing is fine linen and purple.
Her husband is known in the gates
when he sits among the elders of the land.
She makes linen garments and sells them;
she delivers sashes to the merchant.
Strength and dignity are her clothing,
and she laughs at the time to come.
She opens her mouth with wisdom,
and the teaching of kindness is on her tongue.
She looks well to the ways of her household
and does not eat the bread of idleness.
Her children rise up and call her blessed;
her husband also, and he praises her:
'Many women have done excellently,
but you surpass them all.'
Charm is deceitful, and beauty is vain,
but a woman who fears the Lord is to be praised.
Give her of the fruit of her hands,
and let her works praise her in the gates"* (Proverbs 31:10–31)

The Proverbs 31 woman was a trailblazer. Here's what we can learn about her from this description.

She was a real estate developer. She bought a piece of raw land, which suggested she understood investing principles. In a time when women didn't buy land, she developed the land and turned it into a vineyard and created a business.

She was a successful businesswoman. She tilled the land, managed it, and hired people to help. She's referred to as a virtuous woman. She had good integrity and was respected in her community. She had a lot of value. It says she was worth more than rubies. She knew her value in the world. She didn't worry about not being worth the price she needed to charge, not being worthy or deserving of living a full, amazing life full of business and motherhood. She understood her worth and her value.

She was trustworthy. She believed in enrichment. What can you give to make others rich? She understood the call to contribute. She made good use of her talents. She was resourceful. She created plans, which meant she was intentional and set goals. She delegated, which showed that she knew she couldn't do it by herself. She knew she needed a village. She was a hard worker. She had high levels of energy. Her dealings were profitable. She understood the importance of creating a profitable business.

She wasn't lazy. Proverbs 16:27 states, *"Idle hands are the devil's workshop."* She was constantly busy and productive. She opened her hands to the needy. She was confident. She took care of her appearance, which I know is a sore subject in our current day and age. She wasn't keeping up with the Kardashians or living a picture-perfect Pinterest life. That's not what the virtuous woman was, but she knew she was worthy of caring for herself. She didn't feel unworthy of wearing nice things. She understood self-care. It says that she married someone who was equally yoked, driven, positive, and productive to society. She married someone who matched her energy, who matched her goals.

It talks about how she makes things and sells them. Guess what? She's not afraid to sell. She's not afraid to charge what she's worth. She's not afraid to take her talents and find a way to create value for customers that would turn into profits. It talks about how she wasn't just beautiful on the outside, but inside, she was full of strength and dignity. She was motivated. She was positive. She wasn't a complainer. She wasn't a victim. She was wise. She was a good manager and a steward. She made her husband and her children proud.

I could fill an entire book of stories of women who have blazed a trail, who've shown us what's possible.

Can you think of a trailblazer who inspires you? Who's doing what you want to be doing? What kind of character traits do you find valuable when watching that person?

It's time for you to become the trailblazer. The one who is going to pave the way for generations to come. It's going to require you to make a decision. It's more than a choice. You have to make a decision that requires you to commit. I heard an incredible speech at an event where Myron Golden shared some powerful insight into what it means to make a decision and commit to your dreams. The word decision comes from the Latin word "decidere," which is a combination of two words: de (off) and caedere (cut). When you make a decision, you're cutting off any other choices or paths that you could take. You're declaring that this is the choice. You've got to make decisions, not choices. To be clear about what you want, declare that, and move on to it, you must decide. This decision is what's going to provide clarity and free you from the endless "Which path should I take?" Making decisions helps you work past the distractions and the "shiny object syndrome." If you want to get anywhere in life, you have to make decisions instead of constantly entertaining all the possible choices.

Many of us get stuck in information overload. Many of us get stuck in "shiny object syndrome." We look at what others are doing and are constantly bombarded with ideas via marketing and scrolling social media. You watch some family renovate an old bus, and all of a sudden, you have the urge to live as a nomad in a van and travel the world. Then next, you see someone talking about how much money coin-operated laundry businesses make, and now you want to own a laundromat. You see someone else declaring, "Cryptocurrency is the next gold rush!" so you buy a course on that and start dabbling yourself. You see another person show off their weekly sales, detailing how much money they made on a simple PDF download. Do you know how to use Canva? Maybe you should create a PDF and start selling it. I think we can all agree that the world is full of ideas, opportunities, and paths to be successful.

> **We don't lack innovation; we lack execution.**

We end up getting so overwhelmed and distracted we either don't do anything or we do too much at once.

For much of my life, I always envied people who knew what they wanted from a really young age. Walt Disney, for example, was drawing cartoons in his barn as a child. I have always envied that he had this one clear path, this passion and talent, and he had pursued that path his whole life. But for some of us, that's not the story. Most of us spend most of our life wondering about all the possibilities. Drifting and constantly asking, *What is my purpose in life?* or *What should I do? I don't know what I am good at.* We question everything about our skills, our talents, our circumstances, our jobs. For many of us, it isn't so black and white because we struggle with limited beliefs, understanding our own personal capabilities, and lack of motivation. But once you make a decision, the gift you get is clarity. You start making clear choices instead of entertaining endless possibilities.

When you decide to go all in on your life, goals, dreams, and calling, you can't go back. It doesn't mean you only have to do one thing for the rest of your life, but if you don't do something, you will never accomplish anything. It's OK to try something and decide you don't want to do it anymore, or maybe you discover you aren't good at it. Permission to pivot! You aren't trapped in a box or tied to a singular career title. You don't need to let the limits of others hold you down, but you have to stop resisting yourself and break the cycle of indecision. You get one beautiful life; make the most of it. Jump in the boat and burn the bridges behind you. You aren't going backward.

"But Janine," I hear you say, "I really don't know what I want to do or what I am good at?"

When God appeared to Moses and declared that He would use him to lead the Israelites out of Egypt, we know that Moses was reluctant. He didn't feel qualified, yet he grew up as a prince in Egypt. After fleeing to Midian, he spent 40 years tending to his father-in-law's flock. Who better to lead millions of people than a shepherd who tended to his flock faithfully and someone with a unique relationship with Pharaoh? Moses not only had the ability, but he had 80 years of experience. *"The Lord said to him, 'What is that in your hand?' He said, 'A staff'" (Exodus 4:2).*

God used the very tool that Moses had in his hand to create signs of wonders. Your purpose and calling is directly linked to your God-given gifts and abilities. What is in your hand? What gifts, talents, and abilities are in your hands that you can use for His glory?

If you struggle to answer this question, I encourage you to seek counsel, ask those around you, pray, and ask God to help reveal it to you. Sometimes, the very gifts we have seem ordinary to us, and therefore, we don't see them as unique gifts or talents. Ask your spouse, close friends, co-workers, and family members what you are uniquely good at. I did this once and posted it on social media. The response was overwhelmingly beautiful. I didn't realize what people saw in me, and there were so many common themes and gifts that people could see in me that I simply didn't see in myself or consider as anything particularly unique. It set me on a path to using those skills and gifts today. Searching for your purpose can feel like a lifelong pursuit, but it's simpler than you think.

Matthew 7:7 says, *"Ask, and it will be given to you; seek, and you will find; knock, and it will be opened to you."*

All of these first require you to take action. It says, *"Ask, and it will be given to you,"* not *"The answer will find you."* It says, *"Seek, and you will find,"* not *"Wait, and it will come to you."* And it says, *"Knock, and the door will be opened to you"*—it's not an open door you simply stumble across by chance.

You won't always feel motivated or have the clarity you want at any given moment. It's not something that strikes you or that you wait for. You have to have movement and take action, which leads to motivation and clarity. Some of you are waiting on the Lord to make all the moves, and in your waiting, you can't see what He has given you along the way.

The Drowning Man

A fellow was stuck on his rooftop in a flood. He was praying to God for help.

Soon, a man in a rowboat came by and the fellow shouted to the man on the roof, "Jump in. I can save you."

The stranded fellow shouted back, "No, it's OK. I'm praying to God, and He is going to save me."

So the rowboat went on.

Then, a motorboat came by. The fellow in the motorboat shouted, "Jump in, I can save you."

To this, the stranded man said, "No thanks, I'm praying to God, and He is going to save me. I have faith."

So the motorboat went on.

Then a helicopter came by, and the pilot shouted down, "Grab this rope, and I will lift you to safety."

To this, the stranded man again replied, "No thanks, I'm praying to God, and He is going to save me. I have faith."

So, the helicopter reluctantly flew away.

Soon, the water rose above the rooftop, and the man drowned. He went to Heaven. He finally got his chance to discuss this whole situation with God, at which point he exclaimed, "I had faith in you, but you didn't save me; you let me drown. I don't understand why!"

To this, God replied, "I sent you a rowboat and a motorboat and a helicopter; what more did you expect?"[27]

Perhaps God has answered you and provided the vehicle for you to prosper and thrive. My guess isn't that you don't know what to do with it, but that you don't feel worthy of it.

I can tell you right now that there isn't any amount of money in the world that can make you feel worthy. Feeling worthy isn't something that comes with wealth, success, or accolades. Worthiness comes from your ability to love yourself just as your Creator loves you. It's self-acceptance, being more gentle and forgiving with yourself, and simply knowing you are enough.

Only when you know what you are worth will you allow yourself to become who you were always created to be.

In Ephesians 4:1, Paul urges us *"to live a life worthy of the calling you have received."* Paul is sharing what our day-to-day lives should look like if we are walking in faith with the Lord and the gifts God has given. God is asking us to live a life that is consistent with who He is.

I don't know about you, but those are some pretty limitless shoes to walk in. We serve a God so big, gracious, creative, and full of love and light. So help me understand how living small honors Him at all? How does dimming or hiding your light align with God's character?

Becoming a trailblazer requires you to adopt a new identity. It requires you to accept that you are worthy of this life and all God has to offer you. Being a trailblazer isn't comfortable; it requires you to live in your war zone to take massive imperfect action. You will be required to lead, set an example, and pave the way for others. It requires you to stop looking to the left and right and comparing your call to adventure or your path to someone else's. Becoming a trailblazer requires you to use your blessings to help others because you are called for contribution.

Abraham Harold Maslow was an American psychologist, and in 1943, he wrote a paper called "A Theory of Human Motivation." He talks about how our actions are motivated by the desire to meet specific needs. Only when a set of needs is satisfied do we move on to the next. He identifies five sets of needs. First, we start with basic physiological needs: food, water, warmth, rest, and shelter. If we apply this to our financial life, this is money for food, our rent or mortgage, money to keep the lights on—the basic necessities that meet those physiological needs.

The second need is safety. We need to feel secure and protected. The third need is social. We need this sense of belongingness, love, and friendships. We are social beings who need respect, family, and relationships. The fourth need is self-esteem. He talks about your lower esteem and your higher esteem. He mentions that if you meet your lower esteem needs but you don't meet your higher esteem needs, this can lead to "imposter syndrome." And the fifth and top need, once we've met all of those other needs, is self-actualization. This is living according to one's potential, feeling like we've lived out the fullest life that we possibly could. This is at the top of Maslow's Hierarchy of Needs.

I like to think of this self-actualization as fulfilling our purpose and reaching the trailblazer summit. It's the point when we realize we made it and have a 360-degree view of our accomplishment and impact. We cannot reach this summit until all of our other needs have been satisfied in order.

Now, of course, your motivation is constantly changing, and your circumstances, personal growth, and the season that you're in are going to shift these needs and desires. But we're always going to have these needs. We're always going to feel the need to provide for ourselves and our family, make sure we're safe, and make sure that we have good relationships and good, inspiring, positive people in our lives. We're gonna want to live in our higher selves, and we're gonna want to live out our fullest potential.

You're not going to like me saying this, but to become a trailblazer is going to require you to be a little selfish at first. That probably feels uncomfortable. The "Poverty Mind" just stepped in and said, "Whoa, this girl is telling me to be selfish! She's a bad person." But just like the flight attendant says on every safety announcement, "Put your own oxygen mask on first, before assisting others."

To help others, you must first help yourself. When it comes to money, you must build a stable financial foundation for yourself first if you want to be able to adequately assist others. I'm talking about the big picture. I'm not saying you should not give or bless others until you are wealthy. There are many ways you can help others by giving resources like your time, mentoring, or service in your community. I'm saying that you can't help others from a position of weakness. If you are struggling more than they are, you won't be very effective. If there's no oxygen in the plane and you can't breathe, you won't be a hero. You'll just be another casualty.

If you want to contribute, give back to the causes you love, and build a strong financial future for you and your family, it starts with getting your own house in order first.

Many people with a poverty mindset actually believe they are better people because they are poor and that this somehow makes them more righteous or good. T. Harv Eker asks, "What good do you do for poor people by being one of them? Whom do you help by being broke? Aren't you just another mouth to feed? Wouldn't it be more effective for you to create wealth for yourself and then be able to really help others from a place of strength instead of weakness?"

I'm on a mission to help more women build financial strength because I truly believe more money in the hands of women will change the world, and it starts with you, one trailblazer at a time.

The question I hear all the time is, "Do you think God wants you to be rich?" To this, I always reply, "Do you think God wants you to be poor?"

I don't think God wants us to squander opportunities and dim our light to make others comfortable. These are not the attributes of God. God wants you to live a rich, abundant, and full life. Whether or not you believe it is another thing. He says, *"Whoever can be trusted with very little can also be trusted with much. And whoever is dishonest with very little will also be dishonest with much"* (Luke 16:10).

He's shaping your character. He's testing your resilience. He understands your identity, even when you don't. You are a child of God who is called, who is unique, who is loved, who is worthy.

He's calling you trailblazer. It's time to blaze your trail.

CONCLUSION

This is Your Story

Dear Trailblazer,

This chapter is for you. I don't want this to be another book that sparks inspiration only to be consigned to your bookshelf to collect dust. I want this book to move something deep inside of you. If you have made it this far, I know you have a desire for something bigger in your life, and you're ready for your financial life to catch up.

So don't put this on your shelf yet. It's time to take action. Like, right now...

It's time to take radical responsibility for your "money life." Barbara Stanny wrote, "Money without responsibility is like a house of cards. One strong wind, one big crisis, and it all comes tumbling down. Even if nothing happens, even if all goes smoothly... there is always a gnawing fear, unconscious though it may be, that whenever there is the slightest breeze, it may all blow away."

Whether you like it or not, something will change for better or worse. It's time to take back your financial power and take action towards a more prosperous life. Use this chapter to identify your desires, reflect, take massive imperfect action, and create a vision so big it scares you. For years, I have been writing down my dreams and asking myself these questions to help move me to clarity. I hope you make some amazing discoveries, lift your desires to God, and know He is providing and preparing you for such a time as this.

It's time to rewrite your story and give yourself permission to prosper.

Get out a pen, or use your computer if you want. Answer these questions on the next few pages honestly and openly. And if you really want to see these answers come alive and make some serious traction in your finances and life, do these exercises with a friend, spouse, or small group.

I'm rooting for you and can't wait to see what transformation comes from taking this time to take massive action. You've got this!

Prospering Together,
OXOX
Janine

DESIRES:

What does a rich and prosperous life *look* like?

_____
_____
_____
_____

What does a rich and prosperous *feel* like?

_____
_____
_____
_____

If money was no object, what would you do with it? Be as detailed as you can. What would you buy? Who would you want to help? Where would you want to invest?

_____
_____
_____
_____

How will your being wealthy impact others?

_____

_____

_____

_____

_____

Do you feel worthy of wealth? Why or why not?

_____

_____

_____

_____

_____

What fears do you have around money?

_____

_____

_____

_____

_____

Are these fears true, relevant, or helpful? How can you overcome these fears or use them to motivate you?

_____

_____

_____

_____

Can you recognize a money habit or pattern in your life that is holding you back?

_____

_____

_____

_____

RECONCILIATION:

What is one of your earliest memories of money?

_____

_____

_____

_____

How has that memory shaped what you heard, learned, or experienced?

_____

_____

_____

_____

_____

What lesson would you give your own child about money?

_____

_____

_____

_____

_____

What poverty mindset belief do you NOT want to pass on to the next generation?

_____

_____

_____

_____

_____

Fill in the blank:
I am grateful for money because _____
I am grateful for money because _____
I am grateful for money because _____
I am grateful for money because _____
I am grateful for money because _____

You did it! You know how I know you are serious about your financial transformation? Because you did the thing that 98% of people who read this book will never do: the work. It's challenging to be expanded, to face past trauma, to confront your relationship with money, and to dream so big it scares you. Remember, God-sized plans call for God-sized dreams!

I'm a big believer in prayer and I want to end this book unconventionally and in true trailblazer fashion because I'm calling for God-sized transformation and Kingdom revelation over your life and your finances.

Will you pray this prayer over your finances?

"In the name of Jesus, I pray that this will be a breakthrough year for my finances. I pray for divine increase. I pray, Lord, that you will open the floodgates of Heaven and pour favor over my life and my family. I pray for your guidance, provision, and opportunities to steward what you are preparing for me. I thank you in advance for your blessings. I pray that my bank account will overflow so I may bless others in need because I know your blessings are meant to be a blessing. Remove my fear and doubt, and deliver me from the poverty spirit. Fill me with your peace. I am open to receiving your abundance, and I trust in your limitless blessings. In Jesus's name. Amen."

THANK YOU FOR READING MY BOOK!

Because I know you are a doer, I have a special gift just for you. Scan the code below for a few free bonus gifts; no strings are attached! Thank you for trusting me with this journey and for showing up for yourself.

DOWNLOAD YOUR FREE GIFTS

To Download Now, Visit:

I appreciate your interest in my book and value your feedback. I would appreciate it if you could leave your invaluable review on Amazon.com. Thank you!

LET'S CONNECT!

WWW.JANINEMIX.COM

@JanineMix

facebook.com/JanineMix

@janinemix

Permission to Prosper

References

1. Deaton, Angus, and Daniel Kahneman. "High Income Improves Evaluation of Life but Not Emotional Well-being." Princeton University, August 2010. www.princeton.edu/~deaton/downloads/deaton_kahneman_high_income_improves_evaluation_August2010.pdf.

2. Empower. "Can Money Buy Happiness?" (n.d.).

3. https://www.empower.com/the-currency/money/research-financial-happiness.

4. Consumer Financial Protection Bureau. "What Is a Fiduciary?" July 30, 2020. https://www.consumerfinance.gov/ask-cfpb/what-is-a-fiduciary-en-1769/.

5. Bull Oak Capital. "Why You Need to Work with a Fiduciary Financial Advisor." Accessed April 4, 2023. https://bulloak.com/blog/why-you-need-to-work-with-a-fiduciary-financial-advisor.

6. S&P Dow Jones Indices. SPIVA U.S. Scorecard: Year-End 2021. 2022. https://www.spglobal.com/spdji/en/documents/spiva/spiva-us-year-end-2021.pdf.

7. UBS. "UBS Reveals Top Reason Married Women Step Aside in Long-term Financial Decisions: They Believe Their Husbands Know More." WM Americas News, May 14, 2018. https://www.ubs.com/global/de/media/display-page-ndp/en-20180514-ubs-reveals-top-reason.html.

8. Nasdaq. "Generational Wealth: Why Do 70% of Families Lose Their Wealth in the 2nd Generation?" October 19, 2018. https://www.nasdaq.com/articles/generational-wealth%3A-why-do-70-of-families-lose-their-wealth-in-the-2nd-generation-2018-10.

9. Dickson, John. "5 Minute Jesus: The Women Who Bankrolled Jesus' Mission." Undeceptions. (n.d.). https://undeceptions.com/history/5-minute-jesus-the-women-who-bankrolled-jesus-mission/.

10. U.S. Bureau of Labor Statistics. "Occupational Employment and Wages, May 2023." Accessed June 3, 2024. https://www.bls.gov/oes/current/oes212099.htm.

11. Church Law & Tax. "How Churches Spend Their Money." Accessed June 3, 2024. https://www.churchlawandtax.com/manage-finances/budgets/how-churches-spend-their-money/.

12. Wikipedia. "The Salvation Army." Accessed June 3, 2024. https://en.wikipedia.org/wiki/The_Salvation_Army.

13. Focus on the Family. "God's Design for Marriage." Accessed April 4, 2023. https://www.focusonthefamily.com/marriage/gods-design-for-marriage/.

14. Henrich, Joseph, and Mark Muthukrishna. "The Origins and Psychology of Human Cooperation." *Nature Human Behaviour* 5, no. 4 (2021): 409–417. https://doi.org/10.1038/s41562-020-01031-2.

15. Scutti, Susan. "Men and Women Process Emotions Differently, Study Says." *CNN*, October 9, 2017. https://www.cnn.com/2017/10/09/health/gender-differences-giving-receiving-study/index.html.

16. Edelman Financial Engines. Wealth in America 2022: The Path to Prosperity. 2022. https://www.edelmanfinancialengines.com/wealth-in-america-2022/.

17. Cagnassola, Mary Ellen. "This Map Shows How Much Couples in Every State Spend on Weddings." *Money*, May 30, 2023. https://money.com/average-wedding-costs-map-by-state/.

18. U.S. Census Bureau. "Census Bureau Releases New Estimates on America's Families and Living Arrangements." November 17, 2022. https://www.census.gov/newsroom/press-releases/2022/americas-families-and-living-arrangements.html.

19. Lake, Rebecca. "Average Savings by Age." *Forbes*, November 14, 2023. https://www.forbes.com/advisor/banking/savings/average-savings-by-age/.

20. Pye, Jake. "Wedding Debt Is Up and Traditions Are Out." *Debt.com*, January 6, 2024. https://www.debt.com/news/wedding-debt-average/.

21. Davis, Megan, Dana Shepard, and Paul Huang. "Survey: Taking on Debt to Cover Wedding Costs." *LendingTree*, April 10, 2023. https://www.lendingtree.com/debt-consolidation/bridal-party-wedding-survey/.

22. "Value of $30,000 from 1998 to 2023." *In2013Dollars.com*. Accessed July 17, 2024. https://www.in2013dollars.com/us/inflation/1998?amount=30000.

23. Olson, Jessica G., Scott I. Rick, Deborah A. Small, and Eli J. Finkel. "Common Cents: Bank Account Structure and Couples' Relationship Dynamics." *Journal of Consumer Research* 50, no. 4 (2023): 704–721. https://doi.org/10.1093/jcr/ucad020.

24. Gladstone, Jessica J., Emily N. Garbinsky, and Cassie Mogilner. "Pooling Finances and Relationship Satisfaction." *Journal of Personality and Social Psychology* 123, no. 6 (2022): 1293–1314. https://doi.org/10.1037/pspi0000388.

25. Theology of Work Project. "Calling & Vocation (Overview)." Accessed March 20, 2024. https://www.theologyofwork.org/key-topics/vocation-overview-article.

26. Taylor, Bill. "What Breaking the 4-Minute Mile Taught Us about the Limits of Conventional Thinking." *Harvard Business Review*, March 9, 2018. https://hbr.org/2018/03/what-breaking-the-4-minute-mile-taught-us-about-the-limits-of-conventional-thinking.

27. Faulhaber, Markus, Enrico Pocecco, Martin Niedermeier, Gerhard Ruedl, Daniela Walter, Roland Sterr, Hans Ebner, Wolfgang Schobersberger, and Martin Burtscher. "Fall-related Accidents among Hikers in the Austrian Alps: A 9-year Retrospective Study." *BMJ Open Sport & Exercise Medicine* 3, no. 1 (2017): e000304. https://doi.org/10.1136/bmjsem-2017-000304.

28. TruthBook. "The Drowning Man." (n.d.). https://truthbook.com/stories/funny-stories/popular-stories/the-drowning-man/.

Made in the USA
Columbia, SC
21 May 2025